Country of Origin: United States

Mark Sebastian

Trading Options for Edge

Profit from Options and
Manage Risk Like the Professional Trading Firms

PRESS

ISBN 978-1-5015-1475-3
e-ISBN (PDF) 978-1-5015-0567-6
e-ISBN (EPUB) 978-1-5015-0557-7

Library of Congress Cataloging-in-Publication Data
A CIP catalog record for this book has been applied for at the Library of Congress.

Bibliographic information published by the Deutsche Nationalbibliothek
The Deutsche Nationalbibliothek lists this publication in the Deutsche Nationalbibliografie;
detailed bibliographic data are available on the Internet at http://dnb.dnb.de.

© 2017 Mark Sebastian
Published by Walter de Gruyter Inc., Boston/Berlin
Printing and binding: CPI book GmbH, Leck
♾ Printed on acid-free paper
Printed in Germany

www.degruyter.com

—

Status: Loving Lauren

Acknowledgments

There are a few people without which this book could not have been published; I'd like to start with Jeff Pepper, who believed in this book and threw his weight behind it. In addition to Jeff, I'd like to thank Megan Lester, my tech editors Michael Thomsett and Russell Rhoads, copyeditor, Mary Sudul, and Angie MacAllister and the whole De Gruyter/De|G Press publishing team. Thank you to Bill Luby for his wonderful foreword and Michael and Matt Thompson who wrote Chapter 14. In addition to the team of people that helped make this book possible, I would like to acknowledge some individuals that have pushed me throughout my career to better myself:

My Parents, John and Kathleen Sebastian

My brothers and sisters, Nicole, John, Michelle

My partners in Option Pit and my fund, Adam Paris, Andrew Giovinazzi, and
Sam Harris

My director of operations at Option Pit, Licia Leslie

My trading mentor, Scott Kaplan

The professors that pushed me into this direction within finance,
Dr.'s Shawn and Shell Howton

Catherine Clay and the CBOE Livevol team

My brokerage team at Dash Financial

Mark Longo of The Options Insider

Dennis Chen

My clients that believe in me at Karman Line Capital and Option Pit.

Foreword

With the rise of passive investing, the rapid proliferation of exchange-traded products and factor-based approaches to investing, it seems as if we are on the verge of explaining away almost all of what used to be known as alpha. In such circumstances, active investors can be forgiven for wondering if they are playing an unwinnable game. The traditional investment universe is being eroded, commoditized and shrink-wrapped, with algorithms taking over and humans asked to step aside.

Enter options, the next frontier in investing. Here the playing field is evolving quickly and the dynamics are poorly understood by many, leaving a wide variety of significant opportunities for those who are willing to invest the time and energy to understand the nuances of options.

Mark Sebastian is just the person to help explain why options are the next frontier, how to think about them in the context of the broader investment landscape and point to specific methods to capitalize on the opportunity space.

I have known Mark for almost a decade and during this time he has been a leading thinker, writer and educator in the options world. He and I are both naturally drawn to the volatility aspect of the options space and I have always been impressed by Mark's grasp of the big picture as well as some of the minute details that are critical to understanding the VIX and volatility.

As someone who has spent every day for the past dozen or so years thinking about the VIX and volatility, I like to size up options traders by how they think about volatility and right from our first conversation, I knew Mark had a deep understanding of the intricacies of the volatility space. In fact, I was pleased to see that in *Trading Options for Edge*, Mark takes the time to identify four different types of trading environments corresponding to four different levels of the VIX. Better yet, he explains why each volatility zone presents different challenges and opportunities for the options trader. This volatility zone approach is similar to some of my own work and it is refreshing to see it appear here in Mark's own analytical framework.

Mark runs one options-oriented hedge fund and will soon launch his second options hedge fund. In addition, Mark has provided consulting expertise on options and volatility to a number of hedge funds and in his spare time acts as the go-to source on all things VIX for luminaries such as Jim Cramer.

In his first book, *The Option Trader's Hedge Fund*, Mark focused on various options strategies and the main risk management and execution issues associated with those strategies. This time around, Mark takes a novel approach I believe will appeal to all readers. Instead of using options strategies as the starting point and providing guidance for which types of conditions are more/less favorable for particular strategies, Mark uses market conditions and options analytics as a starting point. Most options traders have favorite strategies that they use over and over again in a wide variety of market conditions – and not surprisingly, see varying results. *Trading Options for Edge* is all about understanding how the edge is different in different market environments, with a particular emphasis on volatility conditions, skew and term structure. In other words, this book teaches readers what to look for in the options market and how to translate that analysis of the market into trading what the market gives you. In short, this is not reasoning from options to preferred setups, but looking at setups and market conditions first, then utilizing the options trades that provide the best edge for those setups.

This distinction is not just an academic one, but should be of critical importance going forward. For the past nine years, we have been in a period of declining volatility and are currently experiencing record low volatility. This trend is about to change and as volatility conditions change, so will the edges for everyone's favorite options strategies. Strategies that have been strong performers as of late are sure to struggle while a new set of options strategies will rise to the top.

Frontiers, by their nature, are difficult to comprehend, challenging to navigate and often fraught with danger. It is precisely because so many struggle on the frontier that there is so much opportunity for those who can master a new and poorly mapped terrain.

I am not entirely sure that Mark is the ideal guide to help you find your way through the Alaskan tundra, but when it comes to options, understanding the intricacies of volatility and knowing which market conditions favor certain setups and options strategies, Mark's is the guide you want to have at your side. With *Trading Options for Edge*, Mark turns the tables on traditional options analysis with a top-down approach that is ideally suited to changing market conditions and navigating to the best options trades for each and every market environment.

Embrace the frontier and enjoy the journey!

Bill Luby
Chief Investment Officer, Luby Asset Management
Publisher, VIX and More (VIXandMore.blogspot.com)
October 2017

Contents

Preface

Why am I writing this book? That is the question that my wife, my co-workers, and my friends have asked me. The answer: There are many great books that explain what an option is, how they function, and what the P&L payoffs are for options both bought and sold. There are many books that then take this a step further and walk through what each type of spread is and how to build each of the spreads. These books tend to walk through the P&L payout and may delve into the basic reasons why a trader would put one of the spreads on. Yet there are no books that I have found that adequately explain how these spreads can fit together and the optimal conditions that each of these spreads should be executed under. Essentially, there are a lot of books that can tell you what each option position is and how it makes money. But there are very few, if any, books that explain why a trade should be entered and the optimal conditions for each spread. Even more so, I am not sure there is a book that puts these spreads together so that a trader can tell when to pick a spread. My goal is to fill that void and teach traders how each position works and more importantly how to put several positions together to build a portfolio.

Now that we established why I am writing this book, let me discuss what I want you to learn by reading this book. In short, the answer is conditional trading. But what is conditional trading? Conditional trading is the art of understanding what the market looks like right now and how to trade that market. In essence, while most books are happy to teach you the 'how to build' portions of individual trades, there are no books (that I am aware of) that teach the why of executing a trade, when to enter that trade, and most importantly how to piece all of these trades together.

In this book I am going to show you why you would enter one trade over another. What are the exact conditions when you should trade a butterfly? What are the conditions that make a condor or straddle a great trade? When do you buy premium and when do you sell premium? If you want to buy or sell, what is the best trade for the market right now given the market conditions and the conditions in the stock, ETF, or index itself?

Then I am going to take things one step further by explaining how to piece a portfolio of trades together. If you already have on a butterfly and conditions are ripe for another butterfly, what should you do? As the market changes on a portfolio of trades, how do you add to a portfolio? Can you build a portfolio that can make money most of the time and not get completely run over in the event of a major market collapse like the ones we saw in 2008, 2011, and in August of 2015?

Once a portfolio is built, how should each of the trades and the portfolio be managed? What adjustments make sense in order to minimize losses while ensuring that good money isn't just dumped after bad? How do you make sure that the dollars being spent to manage trades are being implemented in the best way possible?

Finally, I'll discuss the right way to manage and hedge a portfolio for both active traders and for those looking to hedge a portfolio of trades. I'll discuss how constant hedging and 'crisis alpha' are different and how to implement both.

At the conclusion of the book, readers should have a clear idea of not only how the Option Pit Strategy Letter is written and managed by our pros, but how Karman Line Capital, my hedge fund, also manages risk on our trades.

When you have finished this book, my hope is that you will have a clear idea not only what each trade should look like, but what a portfolio of trades should look like.

A small but needed disclaimer, this book is meant for educational purposes only. While I may discuss in general how Option Pit and Karman Line Capital build and enter trades, due to regulatory restrictions this book will not share our performance. Karman Line Capital is offered to qualified investors only on a one-on-one basis. If you have interest, you can contact our CFO directly Adam@karmanlinecapital.com.

I want to thank you in advance for reading this book. I hope you find the time well spent.

Mark S. Sebastian

Introduction

If this is your first options book, you picked up the wrong book. This should be read after you have read books that explain options theory. This book is meant for experienced options traders. Have you been through a 'mentoring' program and been disappointed by your preparedness? Then this is the right book for you. Have you read books by Sheldon Natenberg, Larry McMillian, etc.? Then this book is for you. Have you been trading options for a year or more and understand the Greeks . . . for the most part? Then this book is for you. If your answer was no to any of these, I suggest you go read books that will get you to this point. Then you will be ready to pick up this book. If you still want to buy it, okay, just know that it was written for people with backgrounds in the area. I assume the basics are understood. Once you are ready, here is what you will read:

This book is divided into four main sections:

Part I: Professional Lessons Every Trader Needs to Know

Chapter 1: This chapter will articulate the business side of trading. It then talks through how running a good trading business leads to good risk management. Good books (as in a *book of trades*) mean good understanding of risk. This chapter will explain why.

Chapter 2: This chapter covers the Greeks as they apply to *risk management*. An in-depth discussion of the Greeks as they pertain to market conditions will be covered. Instead of just knowing what the Greeks are, you should understand why the Greeks act the way they do. I will spend LOTS of time on how the Greeks move as market conditions change. Instead of what delta, gamma and vega are, I'll discuss what causes a Greek to change.

Chapter 3. This chapter will cover how market makers manage risk on a position-by-position basis when trading. How do market makers stop themselves from taking on too big of a position for not enough money in a stock or index? This will be your introduction to how I want you to trade.

Chapter 4: This chapter discusses how to evaluate edge trades in terms of volatility. Learn to understand volatility as it relates to realized and implied volatility. Understand the zones that stocks might trade in for a period of time as well as the zones that implied volatility might trade in. Finally, this chapter discusses how the zones relate to one another.

Chapter 5: Here I discuss how to evaluate edge in long and short premium trades. What makes a trade a winner or loser? How do you recognize a good trade from a bad one given market conditions? What part do volatility, term structure and skew play in understanding the particular trade?

Chapter 6: It is not enough to spot edge, you must also capture edge. This chapter is about strategies you can use to capture edge and therefore effectively capture the value. It points out some of the risks that may be associated with a trade that looks too good to be true. It points out how to use a series of trades to lock in edge. It also points out the issues you may have as a retail trader that large houses do not in terms of information and how to actually make the trade to make sure you lock in the value.

Part II: Using Spreads

Chapter 7: This chapter is a survey of the basics of various spreads and conditions where they may be successful. Calls and puts, straddles, strangles, iron butter-flys, butterflys, iron condors, calendar spreads and front and back spreads are covered in this chapter.

Chapter 8: Chapter 8 looks in detail at call and put spreads and how volatility, skew and management of the trade (as in when to get out) enable you to gain edge.

Chapter 9: Similarly to calls and puts, butterflys and condors can be made to gain edge through volatility, skew and management. In this chapter, I present short checklists which point to the best conditions for utilizing these spreads.

Chapter 10: I discuss trading front spreads and broken wing butterflies for edge in this chapter. This will cover how traders manage front spreads, and naked options in a non-directional manner.

Chapter 11: Here I talk about calendar spreads: when to buy them, when to sell them, and when to trade something else. I also discuss how weighted vega affects calendars and where shorts and longs fit within a portfolio.

Part III: Global Risk

Chapter 12: In this chapter I discuss market makers, their role and how they manage risk. Their processes are compared with small traders. Steps taken for rating a trade are presented that should be useful to all traders.

Chapter 13: This chapter discusses book management for the retail and professional customer. I'll show how to engage in net portfolio weighting and how to hold rate trades against a total portfolio. As a portfolio builds into a full set of trades, how do you manage the risk? We examine weighted vega, vol vega, and beta weighting as it relates to a portfolio of trades as well as how to rank a position and how to rank trades.

Chapter 14: This chapter will finish with how a trader can manage catastrophic risk on both long positions and a book of long and short positions—Crisis Alpha. Finally, I'll close with how crashes form, what to look for, and how to manage this risk.

Part IV: Appendices

Appendix A consists of important terms you should be well-versed in for options trading.

Appendix B is a group of blog posts I have written over the years—in real time—as events unfolded. Hopefully by reading what I was thinking during these events (since 2010), right or wrong (I'll note that), you'll understand how a pro might think given a situation of trades.

When you finish reading, I hope many questions have been answered and you are armed with knowledge to help you build a portfolio of trades and how to manage global risk across your book of trades.

Part I: **Professional Lessons Every Trader Needs to Know**

Chapter 1
Trading in Options

This book explains the business of trading options. It is intended for an options trader, or a trader who needs to know more about options trading in order expand trading skills. To fully appreciate the book, you will need a basic grounding in the field, including mastery of options terminology, trading rules, nomenclature, and preferably some preliminary experience in trading options.

An options trader looks at a trade completely differently from a stock transaction. The value judgment in an options trade is limited to *whether* the trade can be made and if there is an 'edge' to the trade (we say a trade 'has edge'). That is, that an options trader knows something about the trade that gives them an edge, or at least perceives a specific advantage based on underlying price movement, option premium levels, and current news (especially earnings surprises or announcements about product approvals, mergers, and other significant changes). If you trade a stock, you make a value judgment about the next direction of price movement; someone on the other end of the trade disagrees with you. The result is that the stock price is an amalgamation of all trading in that stock to arrive at an optimal price. People make trades based on these perceptions, and of course, they can be right or wrong.

Throughout this book, you may find yourself thinking of options trades as "good" or "bad" in the sense of the underlying asset and its current volatility and recent price movement. You might think that the value of the options trade is related directly to the attributes of the underlying security. This is only true to the extent that you know something about the underlying security that may give you an 'edge' in options trading. Throughout the book, this concept of 'edge' is a recurring theme.

The options trading business is about *timing* of transactions. Whether they are smart or not is a different story and, as you will learn, the more volatility in the market, the better it is for options traders. So wise trading may involve resisting the urge to think of options as related directly with whether a stock transaction is a sensible alternative trade. The process involves being able to capitalize on trades, packaging them in combinations, or recognizing hedging opportunities to minimize risk.

The framework for trading options comes from the concept of a *TOMIC* (the one-man insurance company). Traders should approach options just as a large insurance company approaches selling insurance policies to consumers and

https://doi.org/10.1515/9781501505676-001

businesses. In buying and selling options as a TOMIC, you may turn options trading into a business rather than a side activity to investing. The TOMIC approach encourages strong skills in trade selection, risk management, strategy execution, and of course adapting to market conditions as they change. Every TOMIC trader need to understand the basics of this approach before moving into the nuances of trading options for edge.

The TOMIC

Insurance companies make money in two ways, by making a small amount of premium on the insurance they actually sell, and by selling overpriced policies due to greater risks. When selling a policy to a 38-year old male with a wife, children, and a job, the insurance company uses actuarial tables to predict how much it is going to cost to insure a life. While on an individual basis this might cost more than the actuarial table predicts, the insurance company can make money (because the insurance company can write thousands of policies to thousands of individuals and families). Even if the insurance company loses the gamble on a decent minority of those it insures, it will make money. Even outlier events have little to no effect on an insurance company when they write enough policies (generally). The profits are derived from the experience among the insured group at a particular age, as well as by investing reserves throughout a lifetime to earn investment income. While actuarial tables are used for life insurance, other forms of insurance, such as homeowners or automotive, are based on the history of claims in a particular region.

The TOMIC trader is going to take this same approach to writing option policies. For example, as a TOMIC trader, you might decide to sell option spreads at prices that you believe are too high and buy option spreads that are too cheap. This is what an insurance company does as a matter of risk evaluation to arrive at pricing. As a TOMIC trader, you set up a regular routine for trading and executing option trades.

As a TOMIC trader, you develop a process for picking trades while keeping a comprehension of risk and opportunity in mind, typically leaning toward selling option spreads following the guidelines described in later chapters. You set risk limits and capital allocations as a part of this process. Next, you manage the *book of trades*. This process is also described in coming chapters. Then you are able to evaluate the process for following your own trading guidelines (when to enter and exit and how much to place at risk) while constantly looking to improve the process. This requires developing a method for closing trades and taking profits (or accepting losses) systematically to keep dollars in hand. There are other

pieces to the TOMIC philosophy that you will need to master. For example, you will need to manage many forms of risk, such as the risk that an outlier event that can occur. Even this risk can be managed if your trading *book of policies* is put together with risks in mind. In the remainder of this chapter we will discuss the important steps that are necessary to build a successful trading program:
- Build an infrastructure
- Build a trading plan
- Select trades based on articulated criteria
- Manage risks
- Learn all the essential elements of trading

Build an Infrastructure

Every trader, like every organization, has to develop or have access to key infrastructure capabilities that enable the trader to do due diligence. Those capabilities can be costly in both time invested and expense and therefore do not get proper credit. For example, some cost centers on the surface may appear to slow down or interfere with daily work, but upon further study, they are actually centers of efficiency and cost savings. This is the infrastructure of the TOMIC. They are important pieces of every trader's infrastructure. The following infrastructure capabilities should be in place and in use continuously:
- The right clearing firm
- Proper margining
- The right execution platform and executing broker
- The proper analytic tools for volatility analysis
- Risk management tools
- News and information services
- The right hardware
- Proper reporting tools
- A sounding board/risk manager
- A good accountant
- Redundancy of all of the above
- The manager 'got hit' by a bus plan

Only once you have these capabilities in place are you are ready to set up a trading program (your trading business) and begin planning to trade options for edge. Infrastructure will save you thousands of dollars over the years. In addition, a risk manager—a necessary "luxury" many traders forgo, who has little to do with

day to day operations, but is there to make sure you take on the correct risks—
will most definitely make traders more money.

Build a Trading Plan

Trading options for a career, in the TOMIC approach, requires a trading plan. The
first key to a TOMIC trading plan is to take the emotion out of trading. Every trading approach should have a written plan of action. Standard Operational Proce-
dure (SOP) is important when you want to trade like a professional. The process
helps manage things when the plan goes as expected, but it is equally important
that processes are applied when things go wrong—or even slightly off the plan
yet within the realm of possibility. A well-constructed plan prepares for the unexpected. Just as the Navy Seals know what to do when something occurs completely by surprise, a TOMIC trader might not know what to do at the onset of a
crisis, but will know how to determine the proper course of action as the situation
evolves. In all cases, when you deviate from a plan, things go wrong. Improvisation is wonderful . . . in comedy; but in trading and putting money at risk, what
might seem like improvisation is actually derived from a plan. When a basketball
team 'plays on the fly' against a talented, well-coached team, that team loses.
When the team sticks to a plan and a process for evaluating the next play, assuming the team has sufficient talent, that team will win. Even in cases where a dynamic play happens that seems to come out of nowhere, like a fast break, it is
likely the result of good planning on defense or offense. Many of the best traders
know that improvisation is derived from processes and contingencies. Even im-
prov actors that seem to be moving 'on the fly' have an SOP for evaluating what
to do next in a scene, whether they know it or not. This is why the best comedians
study comedy. An effective trading plan doesn't have deviations; it has plans on
how to develop deviations when needed.

A TOMIC plan answers the following:
- What is the normal approach to trading the TOMIC if all goes according to
  plan?
- What is the approach to trading the TOMIC when expected issues happen?
- What is the approach to trading the TOMIC when the unexpected happens?
- How do you analyze conditions when the unexpected happens? How do you
  improvise?

In checking off these questions with a basic approach to trading, you will be able
to stick to a process. When you stick to a process and take emotion out of your

trading, you improve your odds of success. Speaking of emotion, I have seen traders who believe they could do no wrong get burned badly. I have also seen traders who constantly ignore their process because something 'feels' right or wrong. Both typically end up costing the trader money. If you believe that a trade is a good or bad idea, that is one thing, but if you are trading on fear or hubris, the TOMIC approach will fail.

Select Trades Based on Articulated Criteria

Once you build a framework for trading options, you will begin the selection process. This can be tedious and taxing but is worth the investment of time. If you build the appropriate screening process, much like an insurance company screens applicants to fit them to the right risk profile, you can build a screening process for selecting trades. Your screening process of the overall market needs to include:
- Product awareness
- Conditional awareness
- Volatility analysis
- Term structure analysis
- Skew analysis

Once you have analyzed the markets, you next embark on a screening process to select options trades. This involves several steps:

- Evaluate the product to trade

- Evaluate other products

- Determine the viability of a trade

- Pick the trade to execute

- Execute the trade

- Enter the feedback loop

- Look for offsetting or complimentary trades

In combining these steps, you develop a pattern of finding trades that have 'edge' in them, executing them, and then taking profits. In addition, you will be able to build the trading plan using your SOPs.

Manage Risks

Risk management is nothing new. I had a risk manager in my fraternity in college. His job was to make sure our parties didn't turn into unmitigated disasters. He usually failed, but did ensure that we never got into any real trouble. But that's another story. My college itself had a multitude of risk managers. Most corporations have designated risk managers or risk departments. You cannot run a company without an eye on risk. I stress the importance of risk and the need for risk management.

Risk management, in fact, is the most important attribute of trading. It is derived in two ways:

1. *Executing good trades*: If you do not execute profitable trades—those with edge—risk management is a waste of time. One school of options trading states that you can just go out and sell options and you will make money. In theory, over millions of trades, this might be true. However, in the real world, where capital is not limitless, nothing could be further from the truth. The first key to managing risk is to get into trades that have edge. Trades that are executed for edge require less risk management effort. There are typically more dollars per trade, less adjusting, and fewer catastrophic losses.

2. *Managing trades and dollars*: While you can trade options for edge all day, much like an insurance company, some trades will go bad. How you deal with these trades is key. The first key is to have SOPs in place. Proper planning leads to good risk management. However, beyond a trading plan, there are some important considerations to also keep in mind. These include:
   - Asset management
   - Money management
   - Trade allocation management
   - Trade management
   - Outlier risk protection and management
   - Additional addressable risk management

A plan that addresses these considerations ensures your ability to 'trade the next day.' The 'trade the next day' rule means that no matter how bad things get, you will not run out of money to continue trading. Every trader will tell you that the key to longevity is the ability to trade the next day . . . no matter how crazy the market might be. This approach ensures that your trades are properly allocated across a larger portfolio.

Finally, you need to work with a risk manager or, at minimum, a sounding board. At Karman Line Capital, we rely on a risk manager to make sure that the fund stays within in its standard operation plan. In addition, when I choose to improvise it is the risk manager that I use as my sounding board. Giving someone veto power, even over your own money, potentially lowers your net return but dramatically increases your risk-adjusted net profit.

Learn All the Essential Elements of Trading

Every professional needs to undergo a learning process. When I was a floor trader I switched trading pits four times; once when I moved from the AMEX to the CBOE (Chicago Board Options Exchange) and then three different times in six years on the CBOE. In each case, I had to learn a new set of products and rules. When I first left the floor, there weren't even weekly options to trade. Now the range includes weekly options, options on VIX (the CBOE volatility index), weekly options on VIX, you name it. In addition, multiple opportunities to trade in other markets have expanded to include much more, including commodities options on soybeans, even hog options. All of these take time to learn.

When I was hired out of college by Group One Trading, I spent a year learning to trade. Before I traded any products, I spend months observing. In the case of Karman Line, this took years. If you are unfamiliar with a product, consider hiring someone to coach you. At a minimum, find someone you trust to show you the ropes.

Be willing to accept that sometimes conditions change, and the things that made a trade successful can also change. In the late 90's, you could sell any straddle to a customer and win just based on changes in *implied volatility (IV) that options traders believed would occur going forward. This aspect of option pricing at times was* so high that stocks could make wild moves and the options would still be overpriced. Then, in the following decade, this strategy was a net wash at best or a large loser at worst. In 2008, the best trade was the short time spread as volatility fell. Over the next 6 years, the opposite was almost always true; *calendars* (buying an option expiring in one month against selling another option in a different month) had a high success rate. Conditions change and you need to be aware of what is happening around you. At some point a trade might stop working for a time, or permanently. You will develop a sense of when a trade doesn't work and when it might never work again. This can happen.

By constantly educating yourself on what is going on in the market, what other pros are trading, and new products coming on the market, you will be more likely to find yourself on the cutting edge of new trades and products that can make you a lot of money in short periods of time. This points out flaws and potential improvements to an existing strategy. The best traders are constantly learning and improving. Professionals need to have a feedback loop, either through their environment or via one they have created themselves. The purpose of this book is to address and re-address risk management for successful trading and the development of a professional approach to managing your book of options trades.

Chapter 2
Risk Management

In this book, we are going to discuss the ins and outs of risk management. When we talk about managing risks, we are talking about understanding the risk of the positions you take, evaluating them to make sure they are within your policy guidelines, and being able to react to situations that go bad. Risk management is one of the most important keys to trading. Before you start a process of risk management you need to understand the pieces that make up risk management. The key is to understand what the facets of *Greek management* are that allow a trader to manage a position. This means that a trader has to understand the Greeks at a definitive level:

- *Delta* represents the position's sensitivity to changes in an underlying's change in price. A long delta position wants the underlying to rally. A negative (short) delta position profits from a fall in the underlying.
- *Gamma* indicates how the position's delta changes as the underlying moves in one direction or the other. It is often viewed as the rate of change of delta, or mathematically, the slope of the delta curve. Positive gamma will see delta increase if the underlying rallies and fall if the underlying drops. Negative gamma positions will see delta increase as the underlying drops and delta fall as the underlying rallies.
- *Vega* is a measure of how the position makes or loses money as IV changes. If IV changes 1 point, how does the position behave? Does it make money or lose money? A long vega position will profit from an increase in IV, and a short vega position will lose money if IV increases. Similarly, a long vega position will lose if there is a decrease in IV and a short vega position will profit from an increase in IV.
- *Theta* represents how a position makes or loses money as time passes. With the passing of each day, how much is the trader making or losing by carrying the current position? Long theta means that as time passes the trader is theoretically making money. Short theta means that there is a daily cost to carrying the current position that can theoretically cost the trader money. But is that it? The answer is no. The key to risk is to understand how these Greeks and the associated risks change as volatility changes. Volatility changes the outputs of risk control and to really be in control of risk, you have to get how these inputs really work . . . not just what they mean.

https://doi.org/10.1515/9781501505676-002

The Pricing Model

The pricing model for options has five main inputs. While options have been around for 45 years now, the main pieces of the pricing model have never changed. It does not matter whether the firm is Citadel, the leader in advanced option trades, or the average retail trader glued to the screen of a rudimentary brokerage platform. These five factors determine how a trader approaches options:

- Price of the underlying
- Strike price
- Time to expiration
- Cost of carry. For most options trading the cost of carrying is a consideration for levels of dividends (on long positions) or, if margin is used for long positions, the obligation to pay interest.
- Volatility

It is key that you understand what you assume when trading options and use the Greeks to manage your risk—especially for the retail trader, where often the Greeks are set to change with the price of options. While the average market maker can quickly recognize changes in pricing, the standard retail trader cannot. This is because market makers' lives revolve around volatility and staring at screens. A market maker makes money by trading small changes in volatility up and down and against each other. The retail trader has neither the will nor volition to stare at a screen. Additionally, market makers tend to have better analytics, making their task easier. That is not an excuse, just a firm understanding of how volatility behaves with changes in the five Greeks. This is why a trade wins or loses. In the pages that follow, I'm going to spend some time really describing the Greeks. Please refer to Appendix A for brief descriptions of each of the Greeks.

Delta

Delta is the change in price of an option as the underlying price changes. Thus, if an ATM option (*at the money*, usually the most actively traded) has a delta of .50, it will gain 50 cents for every dollar the underlying asset rallies. It will lose 50 cents for every dollar the underlying asset falls. Delta, in most platforms, is a dynamic measure, and can move, not just end of day, but as the day moves along (the change is determined by gamma, discussed in the next section).

We will look at delta in a vacuum. If Option XYZ is trading at 2.50 (in options trader lingo, "trading 2.50") and the underlying XYZ currently trades at $35 per share; XYZ then drops to $34, so option XYZ will be worth 2.00. So, option XYZ would be valued at a lower level per contract if the underlying XYZ fell, with changes reflected point-for-point when ATM.

If Option XYZ is trading at 2.50 and underlying XYZ is trading at $35 and then rallies to $36, option XYZ will be worth 3.00 per contract. If delta was .60, the options would gain 60 cents and would be worth 3.10 on a 1 dollar rally; if .70 it would be worth 3.20 and so on. This is true regardless the size of the contract.

A negative delta will act the opposite way. If the option has a negative delta, it will make money when the underlying falls and lose money when the underlying rallies. In the example above the option would fall to 2.00 on a .50 negative delta option and 1.90 on a .60 negative delta option, etc.

Delta does not care about the underlying price, but relies on the multiplier, how much of the physical underlying each contract expires into. Most options are a 100 multiplier. *However*, there are a few options that have smaller and larger multipliers, especially in futures options. In the S&P 500 E-mini options, the multiplier is 50 not 100. So, an option would only gain 50 * .50 in our example above. The big S&P options have a multiplier of 250, and an option gains 1.25 on a 1.00 move. The calculation for dollars gained or lost is:

*multiplier * delta*

I also use delta as a loose interpretation of percentage chance that an option ends up in the money. Understanding the likelihood of a position moving in the money is valuable when setting up a directional trade.

Do I want a trade that looks for a small move or a large move? If I want a large move, I'll play for a homerun using a low percentage option (low delta). If I expect a smaller move but have some certainty, I move toward a higher delta option to play the percentage. Thus a .60 delta option has a 55–65% chance of ending up in the money, close enough for estimation when doing math in your head, but nothing that should ever be used to directly manage risk.

Seems pretty simple, the concept of delta, but is that it? No, delta is a malleable risk measure that can change. Other factors that affect delta are discussed below. As conditions change in the market, delta changes with the 5 factors that make up the pricing model.

Change in Underlying Price

Some of the factors that move delta are easy to understand and are interrelated with other Greeks. Change in underlying price is the most notable. If I buy a call option that is .50 delta at the $50 strike and the underlying XYZ is trading at $50 per share, then the next week, XYZ moves from $50 to $75 per share, there is *no* way that delta stays at .50, even in the craziest of market situations. An option that was the same price of the underlying that is now 25 points in the money, even in a large cap stock or index, inherently has different odds of being in the money. Think of this like a basketball game. If teams are tied early on and one team takes a 10 point lead, the odds of the team winning with a 10 point lead must increase even if the game is early on. As the underlying price rallies on a positive delta option, the option's delta MUST rise. As the underlying falls, delta must change, in this case lower (as we will see, gamma measures this risk).

When delta is negative, the opposite holds true. When the underlying rallies, the option will become less negative delta. A quick way to view how delta will change is to look at a montage. Take the example in VIX options shown in Figure 2.1:

Delta	IV	Vol	Bid	The	Ask	SIM	Pos	PnL	Last	Strike
70.41	83.96	85.4	3.90	4.04	4.10				3.79	VIX Mar16 20
64.38	87.08	89.1	3.40	3.56	3.60				3.50	VIX Mar16 21
59.43	91.77	93.1	3.10	3.24	3.30				3.10	VIX Mar16 22
53.94	95.33	95.4	2.75	2.83	2.90				2.80	VIX Mar16 23
49.56	98.18	98.1	2.50	2.55	2.60				2.50	VIX Mar16 24
45.79	100.15	101.	2.25	2.33	2.35				2.20	VIX Mar16 25
42.04	102.83	103.	2.05	2.11	2.10				2.00	VIX Mar16 26
38.68	105.42	105.	1.85	1.90	1.95				1.90	VIX Mar16 27
35.68	107.22	108.	1.65	1.74	1.75				1.70	VIX Mar16 28
32.83	109.83	109.	1.50	1.57	1.65				1.55	VIX Mar16 29
30.55	111.28	111.	1.40	1.45	1.50				1.33	VIX Mar16 30

Figure 2.1: VIX screen for March futures trading at 23. On the far left is the delta of the option, the far right is the strike price 'THE' is the "theo" price of the option according to the IV's I was running at the time.

Currently VIX March futures are trading at 23. This screen shows the current deltas for strike prices of 20 to 30. It looks good for making the 20 strike, and that is reflected in the high delta. But as you get to 30 for the strike, the chances are slim and the delta is low. If, in the future, it was to run to 25, in theory the VIX 23 option at 2.80 would have a similar delta to the current 21 strike at 3.50 and the 25 strike at 2.20 should be similar to 23 strike at 2.80, and so on. There are other pieces that affect delta, but one way to see how delta moves is to see the deltas at different strikes.

Change in Strike Price

As the strike changes, so changes the delta of the option. The further from ATM (at the money) the underlying is, the further it will be from delta. Looking at VIX options, refer to the montage in Figure 2.1. With the futures trading 23 in March, the 23 strike in VIX is about a .50 delta (.54 delta to be exact). The 20 is a .70 delta and the 30 strike call is a .30 delta option.

This interaction should be intuitive. Strike prices represent whether the option is in the money, out of the money, or at the money. Of all the facets that affect delta, this one is by far the easiest.

Time to Expiration

The more time it takes for a scenario to occur, the more likely that scenario is to happen. Think about it this way: There is almost no way that the average person is going to stop using Facebook in 2016 or 2017. In 2025, it is entirely possible that no one will use Facebook as a social media outlet. Think I am talking crazy? Remember Myspace had 350 million users at one time.

Let's say AAPL is trading at $150 per share. Could it trade at $200 in 6 months? Probably not. What about a year after it's published? Maybe? What about two years after its published? Entirely possible. The point is, especially with stocks, the longer it takes for something to occur, the more likely something is to happen. Thus, the AAPL 200 call will have a low delta when there is little time to expiration, but in LEAPS (Long-term Equity AnticiPation Securities) it could have a decently high delta.

Volatility

Volatility is the X factor across all Greeks. I am going to spend a lot of time talking about volatility in this book. A simple way to think about the volatility of the option is that it changes *time*. As volatility rises, it makes certain scenarios more and more likely to occur, because it points toward large swings in the underlying. As volatility falls, it points toward different scenarios being less likely to happen.

As volatility rises, it predicts greater movement to follow. Considering volatility is annualized—just looking at an annual move, a $1,000 stock with an implied volatility (IV) of 20% expects the underlying to move higher or lower by 200 points with one standard deviation of confidence. If that $1,000 stock sees its IV increase to 25%, the market now expects a move of 250 points per year, regardless of direction. Since volatility is a function of standard deviation, a stock with a volatility of 16% should move about 1% a day (as the square root of 252 is actually 15.87 which would really be 1%).

The calculation for figuring the standard deviation that the market is currently pricing is:

Underlying price * Implied volatility of the AMT strike * SQRT(trading days to expiration/trading days in a year).

Thus, if XYZ is trading at 20 with IV of 16%, the options market is expecting the underlying to move about .20 a day. A 25 strike call with 30 days to expire is unlikely to end up in the money even if the underlying rallies its volatility number every day.

20 * .16 * SQRT(21/252) = .20

Remember: 30 days to expire means about 21 days of trading, so the market looks for about 3.20 of movement if the underlying went *straight up* over the period of a year.

20 * .16 * SQRT(252/252) = 3.20

Looking at actual volatility over that period of time, taking movement both up and down into consideration, the market is pricing in an XYZ move of 92.

20 * .16 * SQRT(21/252) = .92

The 25's are not expected to end up in the money. They will end up with a ballpark delta of less than 10 and a value of less than .20 per contract given the current time to expiration.

If expectation of movements increases in stock XYZ to 32%, double that of the previous example, all of the sudden the market is looking for 1.84 over a month of movement and if the stock catches some momentum, the underlying could blow through the upside call. Whereas the 25 strike call had a delta of less than 10 and a value less than .20, the option now has new life. The option will have a delta near 20 and a value near .50 per contract. If the IV jumps to 48%, the strike is going to have some serious value. Delta will be over 25 and the option will start to approach at least a 1.00 valuation give or take (.5 * 2x IV).

The view of volatility is much like turning the clock back. A two-year scenario makes outcomes seem more likely to happen, and higher volatility makes scenarios more likely to happen. If I move IV from 16% to 32%, it's like moving days to expiration from 30 (21 days to expiration) to 90 days (63 days to expiration) to expiration. To compare:

$$20 * .16 * SQRT(63/252) = 1.84$$

$$20 * .32 * SQRT(21/252) = 1.91$$

The above are similar even though the days to expiration are different; this is the power volatility has on standard deviation, which determines delta. Nothing will affect the outcome of an option like volatility. To understand a Greek is to understand the effect of volatility.

Gamma

In my experience, *gamma* is the Greek that traders have the hardest time understanding. It's also the Greek most likely to blow the trader up. I can speak from experience; there is no trader that has not been beaten badly by gamma. I have had occasions where an explosion in gamma has made or lost thousands of dollars.

Gamma represents how delta changes with a 1 dollar change in the underlying, regardless of the price of the underlying. Thus, if you trade SPX which is about 2000 dollars per contract, gamma measures change in delta for 1 dollar and the same is true if you are trading SPY which is around 200 dollars. Both are indexes of the Standard and Poor's 500 and yet they have quite different gammas because of the underlying. More importantly, the sign and movement of gamma has *nothing* to do with the delta value. A negative delta can be accompanied by a positive gamma and a positive delta can have a negative gamma.

Let's quickly examine gamma:

XYZ is trading at $30, and a long 30 strike put has a negative delta of -0.5 and a positive gamma of 0.1. If the underlying rallies 1 dollar to $31, the delta will change from -0.5 to -0.4.

XYZ is trading $30, and a long 30 strike call has a positive delta of 0.5 and a positive gamma of 0.1. If the underlying rallies 1 to $31 the delta will change from 0.5 to 0.6.

The sign of gamma does not matter. Looking at the opposite:

XYZ is trading at $30, and a short 30 strike put has a negative delta of -0.5 and a positive gamma of 0.1. If the underlying rallies 1 dollar to $31 the delta will change from -0.5 to -0.4.

XYZ is trading at $30, and a short 30 strike call has a positive delta of 0.5 and a positive gamma of 0.1. If the underlying rallies 1 to $31 the delta will change from 0.5 to 0.6.

This is all well and good. Where gamma becomes dangerous is on a gap move. Look at the examples above and imagine the move was a gap. A *gap* means that you wake up and the underlying opens to where its current price is trading. Let's take an example from above to a possible scenario. Imagine you have a position that is short gamma in XYZ, trading at $125, and the position is flat delta but short gamma to the tune of 0.450 * 10 or 4.50 on a stock with the standard 100 dollar multiplier. The trader is short 10 contracts with a gamma of short 0.40. XYZ opens up one day at $100.

The calculation is:

($\frac{1}{2}$ gamma * change in price squared + delta * change in price) * (contracts * multiplier)

Thus $\frac{1}{2}$(-0.45) * 25 * (10 * 100) = -5625

On 10 contracts, the trade lost over 5600 dollars; this is the power of gamma.

I could switch the signs and all of the above would still work. The process of working through delta and gamma will make the process easier to understand. Of the Greeks, gamma is by far the least intuitive.

Traders obsess about their gamma exposure. This is because, as I stated in the first paragraph of the section, true exposure to movement is really derived.

With the risk associated with gaps, traders have to control how gamma exposes them to movement in the underlying overnight. Additionally, gamma can become a problem for traders if the underlying moves up and down wildly. If an underlying moves up or down wildly throughout the day, the gamma of the position can push delta to change drastically throughout the day as well. I have seen scenarios where a $60 stock opened down $10 only to end up on the day by even more than $10. The intraday movement could cause a trader that is short gamma to have to sell a large amount of the underlying on the bottom to reduce delta exposure, only to have to buy the underlying all the way back up and even up on the day as the underlying moves. In the example above, I showed how a loss of $5,625 can come from a big gap down. In order to protect yourself from the delta exposure created by negative gamma, traders typically sell the underlying to reduce risk. Now imagine the additional losses if the underlying rallies. Not only is the trader locking in $5,625 dollars of loss on the bottom, but would lose another $5,600 or more if the stock ends up flat on the day and the trader did not buy stock on the way up. Even heading the delta dynamically on the way up the trader would lose ½ of $5,600.

My point is that gamma is the risk factor professionals watch more than any other Greek, and for good reason. It is the only Greek that can allow a position to get away from a trader in a way that the P&L loss is unrecoverable. In monitoring gamma, the trader is able to monitor the risk of movement, how the trader is exposed to realized volatility . . . movement in the underlying.

Let's add a new dimension by walking through how the five factors effect gamma.

Price of the Underlying

Recall that the SPX and SPY can each have a gamma of 1. However, a 1-point move in SPX is totally different from a 1-point move in SPY. A 1-point move in SPX trading at $2,000 represents a .05% move in the underlying. Not exactly ground breaking; a business reporter would announce the S&P 500 as unchanged. While not huge, this is a much larger move than what the SPY would experience. A 1-point move in the SPX is barely a nudge in price because the index is 10 times as large as SPY. So, a 1-point move in the SPY would be 10 times more of a move in the underlying (0.5%). Thus, the SPY is going to have 10x the gamma of the same position in SPX. The higher the price of the underlying, the lower the gamma. The higher the price of the underlying, the higher the pure point movement *should* be . . . at least in indexes.

This same concept applies to equity options. A stock like AMZN which is around $995 as of the end of May 2017 may move 1% a day and a stock like NKE which might be trading at $99.50 would move the same with a lower dollar level. If they had the same IVs, the gamma of NKE would be 1/10 of the stock trading at AMZN's level.

Strike Price

Gamma is odd in how it moves. It is at its highest point "at the money." The further the move away from ATM, the smaller gamma becomes, as a general rule. This is pretty simple until you add in the other 5 factors, most notably volatility and movement in the underlying. When the underlying moves and volatility also moves, the gamma of a strike price can change in ways that the trader, if unaware of gamma's power, will be blown away. Options that are sold with low gamma can quickly evolve to a high gamma, because gamma can move a position's delta extremely quickly on a gap. Remember this in all trades, it will save your butt.

Time to Expiration

Recall that the longer time to expiration, the more delta will remain the same. If gamma is the change in delta on a 1-dollar move, then a 1-dollar move matters. When an option has a few days to expire, a 1-dollar move can be HUGE. When an option has a long time to expire, a 1-dollar move might not matter as much. Let's take a quick look:

An underlying is trading at $24 with options expiring in 2 days. If the underlying rallies 2 dollars, the chances of ending up in the money at $25 increase significantly. The calls may go from a somewhat lower delta, say 35, to a somewhat higher delta, say 65. Thus, the change in delta associated with that 2-dollar move might be 30 delta points. This means gamma was about 15.

Look at the same scenario with the 35-strike option. With two days to expire, does a change in the underlying price from 24 to 26 actually affect delta of the 35 strike call? Not really. The 35 strike call might go from 0.02 delta to 0.04 delta, resulting in a gamma of 1.

Looking at an option with 6 months to expire and that same move from 24 to 26, the change is much smaller. It might result in the option premium moving from 47 to 53. Thus, the 2-dollar move caused a change in delta of 6 and a gamma of 3.00, only 1/5 the gamma of the options with 2 days to expire. The point is that increasing gamma may point to higher rewards or greater losses. In some cases, gamma may look like a positive, but in reality, the number just represents swings in the strike chain that may be well out of the money.

It may, as in the preceding example, be dramatically affected by the expiration date. So, in interpreting gamma, look at it with a view at the other Greeks to make sure your interpretation is correct.

Clearly the greater the time to expire, the less gamma that is produced. To see this in a simpler way, pull up a montage of options and examine how different the deltas are at different strike prices in options that are close to expiration versus options not close to expiration. The montage of VXX in Figure 2.2 shows options with 5 days to expire and their deltas.

OI	Volume	Delt	IV	Vo	Bid	Th	Ask	SIM	Pos	PnL	Last	Strike
1544	9240	31.9	73.2	68.	0.44	0.4	0.48				0.54	VXX(W) Feb05 25
6232	2002	24.8	77.2	70.	0.35	0.3	0.38				0.42	VXX(W) Feb05 25.5
210C	2870	19.2	79.6	72.	0.27	0.2	0.29				0.32	VXX(W) Feb05 26
962	4138	14.8	82.5	75.	0.21	0.1	0.23				0.25	VXX(W) Feb05 26.5
1486	995	11.3	85.6	77.	0.16	0.1	0.19				0.19	VXX(W) Feb05 27
635	418	8.79	88.5	79.	0.13	0.0	0.15				0.14	VXX(W) Feb05 27.5
1627	1040	7.00	91.7	82.	0.11	0.0	0.12				0.13	VXX(W) Feb05 28
1132	495	5.38	93.7	84.	0.08	0.0	0.10				0.11	VXX(W) Feb05 28.5
2528	1913	4.27	98.1	87.	0.07	0.0	0.09				0.09	VXX(W) Feb05 29
993	427	3.26	97.2	88.	0.04	0.0	0.07				0.08	VXX(W) Feb05 29.5
2102	737	2.51	103.	90.	0.05	0.0	0.06				0.06	VXX(W) Feb05 30
117	467	2.19	103.	94.	0.02	0.0	0.06				0.06	VXX(W) Feb05 30.5
3811	281	1.73	108.	95.	0.03	0.0	0.05				0.04	VXX(W) Feb05 31
241	342	1.65	114.	10(	0.03	0.0	0.05				0.04	VXX(W) Feb05 31.5
1847	3727	1.24	117.	101	0.02	0.0	0.05				0.04	VXX(W) Feb05 32
99	125	1.19	119.	10!	0.02	0.0	0.04				0.03	VXX(W) Feb05 32.5
189C	837	1.15	124.	11(	0.02	0.0	0.04				0.03	VXX(W) Feb05 33
98	20	0.80	117.	10!		0.0	0.03				0.02	VXX(W) Feb05 33.5
1442	10	0.62	121.	10!		0.0	0.03				0.02	VXX(W) Feb05 34
464	55	0.44	126.	10!			0.03				0.02	VXX(W) Feb05 34.5
1732	209	0.43	124.	11:			0.02				0.02	VXX(W) Feb05 35

Figure 2.2: Note deltas of VXX options with 5 days to expiration and VXX trading around 23.5.

Does it appear that the 35 strike calls will be affected by any 2 dollar move in the underlying? And VXX moves . . . *a lot*! Based on the above, if VXX were to move $2, the 35 delta call *might* pick up .5 points, but almost no gamma.

Now look at a similar set of strikes on options in VXX with 6 months to expire. What that might look like is shown in Figure 2.3.

Delt	IV	Vo	Bid	Th	Ask	SIM	Pos	PnL	Last	Strike
55.3	82.8	83.	4.25	4.3	4.40				4.48	VXX Jun17 25
52.5	84.1	84.	3.95	4.0	4.15				4.30	VXX Jun17 26
49.9	84.8	85.	3.70	3.8	3.85				3.93	VXX Jun17 27
47.4	86.0	86.	3.45	3.5	3.65				3.72	VXX Jun17 28
45.0	86.9	86.	3.25	3.3	3.40				3.40	VXX Jun17 29
42.9	87.8	87.	3.05	3.1	3.20				3.20	VXX Jun17 30
40.7	88.6	88.	2.89	2.9	2.99					VXX Jun17 31
38.8	89.2	89.	2.71	2.7	2.81				3.08	VXX Jun17 32
37.0	89.9	90.	2.55	2.6	2.65					VXX Jun17 33
35.2	90.5	90.	2.33	2.4	2.56					VXX Jun17 34
33.5	92.6	91.	2.24	2.3	2.53				2.36	VXX Jun17 35

Figure 2.3: A montage of VIX call options with six months to expire.

The 33 strike option had a delta of 37, and the 35 was 33.5. Change in delta of the 35 strike will be at least 3.5/2 or 1.75 gamma, or about three times that of the options with a week to expire. Essentially gamma near the money was *super high* relative to the strikes around it. This is because if the underlying moves 1 point, delta would change dramatically as the option approaches expiration.

Volatility

Volatility can act much like time. Running up IV can be like rolling the clock back. At the same time, low IV options have higher gamma than high IV options. If it sounds confusing, then now you understand why this is going to be the longest chapter of this book. Let's start with the simple, low IV stocks versus high IV stocks. Stock XYZ is a low IV stock; its options (regardless of time to expiration) have deltas across strikes as shown in Figure 2.4. Based on delta levels, XYZ is assumed to be trading at or close to $55 at this point.

Strike Price	IV	Delta	Gamma
50	25	65	3
55	25	50	3
60	25	35	3

Figure 2.4: Sample delta and gamma in a hypothetical stock with an IV of 25.

In the example in Figure 2.4, as the underlying moves from $55 to $60, the delta will go to from 50 to 35, a gamma of 3. Now let's pump up the IV a touch in Figure 2.5.

Strike Price	IV	Delta	Gamma
50	35	60	2
55	35	50	2
60	35	40	2

Figure 2.5: IV at sample delta and gamma in a hypothetical stock with an IV of 35.

An increase in IV makes all occurrences more likely, thus you'll notice in Figure 2.5 that deltas have changed. The IV pump increased the deltas of the 50 and 60 strike options. This in turn causes the gamma of each strike to decrease. This is the way things work for ATM options and for options that have a long time to expire. But how does volatility affect OTM options?

Believe it or not, it was a student who taught me the best way to think about OTM options. The student pulled out a stream of options that looked like a normal curve. The normal curve represented delta; he then pulled the string just a bit. What I noticed was that near the peak (which is ATM) the slope decreased (change in slope of a delta curve is gamma). However, at the ends, where the student was actually pulling the strings, the slope increased. See the example of how gamma changes on an OTM call with an increase in volatility.

Take a look at the risk graph in Figure 2.6, notice the change in gamma with a 30% increase in volatility on an option with a delta of about 0.10 (we bought 20 contracts to make the move clear).

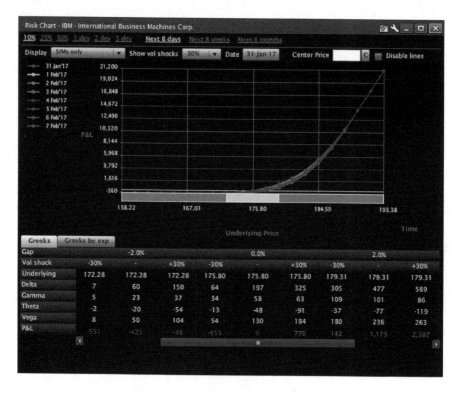

Figure 2.6: The OTM option gamma actually increases in this example.

When an option is *way out of the money*, below a -0.15 delta, and up to a 0.15 delta, the options gamma will increase. Let's look at some OTM options with an increase in IV in Figure 2.7 and Figure 2.8.

Strike Price	IV	Delta	Gamma
80	25	10	0.4
85	25	8	0.4
90	25	6	0.4

Figure 2.7: Delta and gamma of hypothetical OTM options with IV of 25.

The options in Figure 2.7 represent options that are well out of the money. I am going to increase IV and then make up some deltas.

Strike Price	IV	Delta	Gamma
80	35	14	0.8
85	35	11	0.8
90	35	8	0.8

Figure 2.8: Delta and gamma of hypothetical OTM options with IV of 35.

While it might seem insignificant, the gamma of the options above actually doubled from 0.4 to 0.8. This is the danger of shorting OTM options—the gamma can explode; I will go into detail later. Imagine that the above IV moves with an increase in the underlying. Imagine you are short the 85 calls and the underlying moves *with* a drop in volatility? Not only does the short delta change *but* the gamma increases. Now you know how someone can turn a small position into a loser of incredible proportions.

Vega

The *vega* of an option tracks how the option's price moves with changes in implied volatility (IV). Think of it as the delta of implied volatility. If an option is worth 3.00 and has a vega of 1.00, and IV increases one point, the value of the option will be 4.00. Seems pretty simple—but it's not. The nice thing about vega is that relative to gamma it is pretty simple . . . *relative to gamma*. In many ways, vega's characteristics are exactly like the characteristics of delta; the big difference is that the Greek affected is the vega number (IV), not the delta number (underlying price).

Price of the Underlying

In simple terms, the higher the price of the underlying, the more vega it will have. SPX and SPY have essentially the same underlying, the S&P 500; but one represents the full value times 100. The other represents 1/10 of that value. As a result, SPX options have much more vega than SPY options. This is a result of each option being assigned to an underlying with much more value. An option on SPX can be worth 100 dollars or more. An increase in IV of 1 point might be at 5 dollars. That's vega of 5. In SPY, an increase in IV in the same amount might only be 0.50.

This means that SPX has vega of 5 and SPY has vega of 0.50. Compare XSP (mini SPX options) and SPX vegas on similar strikes and expirations in Figure 2.9.

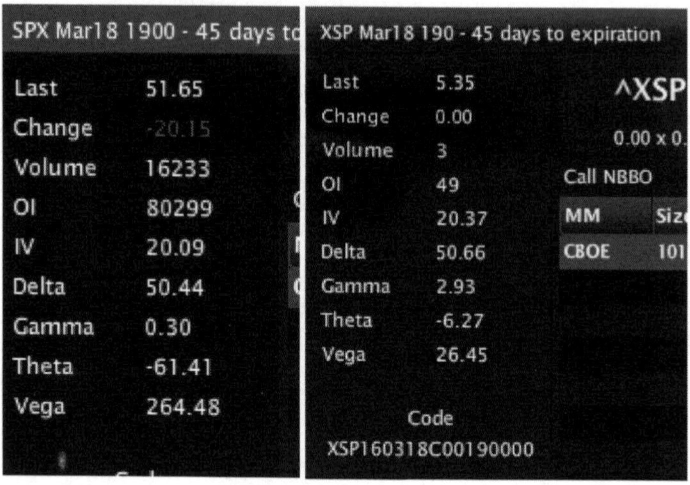

SPX Mar18 1900 - 45 days to	XSP Mar18 190 - 45 days to expiration		
Last	51.65	Last	5.35	^XSP
Change	-20.15	Change	0.00	
		Volume	3	0.00 x 0.
Volume	16233	OI	49	Call NBBO
OI	80299	IV	20.37	**MM** Siz
IV	20.09	Delta	50.66	**CBOE** 101
Delta	50.44	Gamma	2.93	
Gamma	0.30	Theta	-6.27	
Theta	-61.41	Vega	26.45	
Vega	264.48			
		Code		
		XSP160318C00190000		

Figure 2.9: Comparison of vegas of XSP and SPX.

Note in the above, minus a decimal, the vega number would be exactly the same. This is clear evidence that it's all about the price of the underlying when it comes to vega numbers.

Strike Price

The closer the strike price is to the money, the more vega it will have. The ATM options always have a high vega relative to the strikes that are out of the money. The further the strike moves from the underlying, the lower the vega. That doesn't mean that managing vega is easy. Like gamma, vega can explode on a given strike price. The explosion of vega on a short strike, with the explosion of gamma, is what we in the business call a *blowout—the complete inability for a trade to go forward because the clearing firm is forcing the trader to liquidate.* The first rule of trading is that the trader must be able to trade the next day. If a trader blows out, he or she is likely in liquidation-only mode and will be out of a job or out of money. Either way, it's an awful feeling and one that should be avoided at all costs.

Time to Expiration

One thing about volatility is that it does not move fluidly across the spectrum of expirations, sometimes called *term structure*. Options with a longer time to expire are worth more; they always will be. Thus, they have more vega.

In the SPX options in Figure 2.10, the value of the ATM strike increases from about 47.50 up to 62.50 dollars from March to April when the options expire. That extra time premium, represents extra exposure to vega. If you have not made the connection by now, time premium equates to raw vega exposure.

OI	Volume	Delt	IV	Vo	Bid	Th	Ask	SIM	Pos	PnL	Last	Strike	Last	PnL
38 days to expiration														
893	243	50.3	20.1		46.90	47.	48.30				48.10	SPXW(W) Mar11 1900	52.20	
15	9	48.7	19.9		44.00	44.	45.40				42.60	SPXW(W) Mar11 1905	53.90	
45 days to expiration														
8029	16233	50.4	20.0		51.00	51.	52.20				51.65	SPX Mar18 1900	55.30	
1207	7471	49.0	19.9		48.10	48.	49.80				49.70	SPX Mar18 1905	55.90	
51 days to expiration														
52	2	50.6	20.2		55.00	55.	56.20				53.05	SPXW(W) Mar24 1900	60.45	
11		49.2	20.0		52.10	52.	53.20					SPXW(W) Mar24 1905		
58 days to expiration														
2463		50.7	20.0		57.80	58.	59.20					SPXW(W) Mar31 1900	63.00	
2		49.3	19.8		54.90	55.	56.20					SPXW(W) Mar31 1905	61.10	
59 days to expiration														
5		50.6	20.1		58.60	59.	59.90					SPXW(W) Apr01 1900		
		49.3	19.9		55.70	56.	56.90					SPXW(W) Apr01 1905	64.20	
66 days to expiration														
		50.5	20.1		61.70	62.	63.00					SPXW(W) Apr08 1900	62.35	
		49.3	19.9		58.80	59.	60.00					SPXW(W) Apr08 1905		

Figure 2.10: Call options in the SPX across multiple expirations.

The problem is that it doesn't get any simpler from there. Just because an option has more vega does not mean it makes more money when IV explodes. That also doesn't mean they move in the same manner as options with less time to expire. I am going to spend some time discussing this concept in detail later. However, to start let's make one thing clear, an option with 1 month to expire and an option with 6 months to expire will have very different vegas, but the option with 1 month to expire will react to volatility in completely different ways.

If I own an asset that has movement at 25% and that movement increases to 30% near term, options will gain value, but the interpretation of a longer-term option will change too. A longer-term option will gain a much larger amount. This is because the market thinks that the underlying is going to keep moving the way it is moving now. Think about it this way: An option on an underlying for which vol increases from 25% to 30% will see its long-term options change in value, because the market assumes that movement has more increases still to come.

A jump in movement to 30%, even in the short term, must have a ramification on long term movement. If a stock starts flailing around, the long-term plays will pick up a lot of value, all else being equal. From a market-driven perspective, if people are scared, they do not just hedge their position for the next 30 days. Demand for positions in the underlying increases out 3, 6, and 12 months plus. All the way out to the longest LEAP, demand for shares is expected to increase. Banks and trading firms, those providing liquidity to hedgers, need to hedge trades they made with a lot of 'edge' in them that now maybe do not look so hot, this is the source of demand. Banks and trading firms need to follow rule number one (always be able to trade the next day), just like the individual trader. This creates demand in areas that are not being bought by the public, typically the back months.

Volatility

Strike prices that are ATM have the most vega. The further from ATM the strike price is, the less vega there will be. As IV increases, strike price characteristics become more alike. Thus, an increase in vol makes all options more like ATM, which have the most vega. As volatility increases for OTM strikes, they become more like ATM. Hence, volatility affects strike prices by making OTM options increase in vega until they become ATM options. As volatility increases, vega advances.

ATM options are quite simple; volatility can go wherever it wants; as long as it doesn't go infinitely high, ATM vega will be stable.

Theta

Unlike delta, gamma, and to a lesser extent vega, there is no other Greek to tie theta to in terms of movement. Vega tends to move around based on time value, more or less. Theta is tied to gamma in terms of intensity, but not in terms of movement.

Theta is the rate at which an option loses value. Like all insurance products, as time passes an option loses a piece of value. If you buy an option in XYZ with a strike of $30 and pay 3 ($300), and the underlying is trading at $29 per share, if the underlying still trades at $29 at expiration, that option must be worth zero. The process of that option getting to zero, in the days that passed, is what theta measures.

Price of the Underlying

Much like vega, when an underlying is high, options will have a high theta. Going back to our XSP and SPX example, the same thing that produces a higher vega in options produces a higher theta. In Figures 2.11 and 2.12 you can see that an OTM option in SPX relative to XSP is going to be worth about 10 times that of an XSP option.

OI	Volume	Del	Gamma	IV	Vol	Bid	Theo	Ask	SII	Pos	PnL	Last	Las	Strike
16 days to expiration														
18041	8469	54.1	0.96	8.01	8.23	17.50	18.48	18.60				17.0	16.0	SPX(AM) Jun16 2410
19960	1048	49.3	1.00	7.74	7.98	14.50	15.48	15.50				13.7	18.0	SPX(AM) Jun16 2415

Figure 2.11: ATM June options in SPX.

OI	Volume	Del	Gamma	IV	Vol	Bid	Theo	Ask	SII	Pos	PnL	Last	Las	Strike
16 days to expiration														
1091	23	53.9	9.78	8.10		1.59	1.81	2.03				1.74	1.80	XSP Jun16 241
		49.0	10.09	7.89		1.33	1.51	1.70						XSP Jun16 241.5

Figure 2.12: ATM June options in XSP.

Over the next 45 days, the SPX option has 10 times the dollar value to lose. Having 10 times the value means that over the next 45 days instead of losing 5 dollars, the option has to lose 50. Thus, *ceteris paribus*, the higher the price, the higher the theta.

Strike Price

ATM options have the highest premium. These have the highest theta number. In addition, ATM options have the standard theta curve, Figure 2.13, that we are all used to seeing:

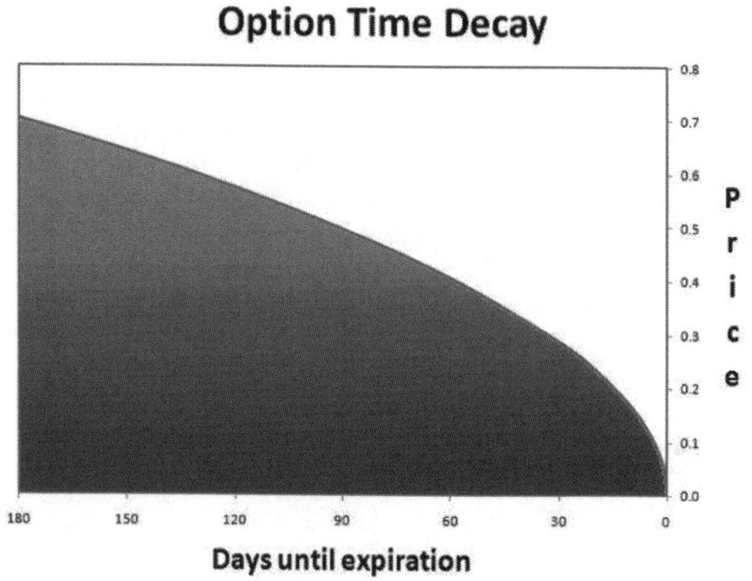

Option Time Decay

Days until expiration

Figure 2.13: The standard theta curve of ATM options.

As time to expiration approaches, ATM options see their theta increase exponentially. With the 30 days having huge theta, and the final 7 days having massive theta getting even higher.

OTM options are not the same. The decay curve for OTM options is much more linear than that of ATM options. As strike becomes more and more OTM, the theta decay becomes more linear. Decay is more linear the further out of the money an option is.

Unit options are options worth very little and far out of the money. For a standard stock, I would expect that a unit option will be worth less than .15 or so. These are options that have no value other than pure catastrophe insurance and they take *forever* to decay. There are two main reasons that these options retain value:

1. Margining: Market makers have their margin assessed in two ways. The more margin market makers have, the more capital is tied up. So, if market makers are trying to be as capital efficient as possible, they will always stay away from selling options that tie up margin by a large amount.

   The SEC mandates that for every option, be it worth .05 or 5,000, the market maker is charged at least .25 per contract. An option worth .05 ties up an inordinate amount of margin for the market maker. If I am short one hundred 5 cent options, I can make 500.00 (.05 * 100 * 100) on the 100 options I am short. At the minimum, even if I am long, I am going to be charged $25 of margin due to SEC rules. That may not be the best engagement of capital.

   The more treacherous effect on margin is *risk haircut*. Clearing firms run an algorithm on a portfolio assessing risk if the underlying moves 10, 20, and up to 40%. A trader who has several of these short option positions can see the cost of owning a position via 'tinnie options' go much higher as .05 options are seen as a serious risk (back in the day 'tinnie options' were described as options worth 1/16 of a dollar or less, now usually they are referred to as options worth less than .10). Additionally, they run risk on increases in volatility of up to 400%. The charge of margin on these options can be astronomically high. If a trader is short 100 .05 options and IV increases 400%, suddenly the 'worthless' out of the money options that were sold at .05 are no longer worthless. Seeing this, the clearing firm must raise the margin requirements by a large amount. Clearing firms, understanding the risk potential, do not wait for vega to explode; they margin some of this risk into the options from day one. This makes being short these options potentially as expensive as the premium collected. Putting up large amounts of capital to make $500 is not what traders typically try to accomplish. Being short cheap options is not an efficient use of capital. This is going to slow the rate of decay in ways that the option pricing model cannot measure.

2. The actual risk reward is the other issue with units. If you are a bottomless pit of money, you expect the value of shorting an option worth .05 to be high; they often end up worthless. However, most traders are not bottomless pits of money. The ability to make $500 on a $100 lot that is 99% likely to win, does not counteract the risk of loss, say $25,000 once, even if it has a positive expectation. Major firms don't care about these type of losses, but the average retail trader does.

When I was interviewing candidates at Group One Trading, we asked college kids if they would risk 500,000 dollars on a coin flip if they could win 1 million dollars if they were right. If they said yes, they were unlikely to get a job. We simply did not have that kind of risk appetite; neither do most market making firms, except those with the deepest pockets. The 'risk appetite' effect on small options keeps them bid higher for longer. This slows the decay in these options beyond what the pricing model expects. Based on values in GE (General Electric) options in Figure 2.14, the 27.5 puts lost more value between week 3 and week 2 then they did from week 2 to week 1. This is the 'unit effect,' the idea that once an option hits a specific value its rate of decay breaks from the pricing model and slows to a crawl. Once an option hits its unit effect level, the cost of being short tends to become a bad trade for the average trader.

Strike	Last	PnL	Pos	SIM	Bid	The	Ask	Vol	IV	De	V
GE(W) Feb05 27.5	0.03				0.02	0.04	0.05		44.	8.5	3
GE(W) Feb05 28	0.08				0.05	0.06	0.08		35.	16.	3
GE(W) Feb05 28.5	0.18				0.16	0.18	0.20		32.	39.	7
GE(W) Feb05 29	0.51				0.41	0.44	0.48		29	71.	3
GE(W) Feb05 29.5					0.80	1.13	1.46		77.	69.	
GE(W) Feb05 30					1.29	1.72	2.15		11(	71.	
GE(W) Feb12 27.5	0.15				0.10	0.11	0.13		28.	16.	1
GE(W) Feb12 28	0.20				0.19	0.20	0.21		26.	27.	1
GE(W) Feb12 28.5	0.35				0.33	0.35	0.37		24.	43.	5
GE(W) Feb12 29	0.65				0.57	0.62	0.66		23.	61.	1
GE(W) Feb12 29.5					0.87	1.04	1.21		28.	73.	
GE(W) Feb12 30					1.29	1.61	1.93		41.	74.	
GE Feb19 27.5	0.26				0.22	0.24	0.27		27.	24.	4
GE Feb19 28	0.40				0.35	0.38	0.41		25.	35.	1
GE Feb19 28.5					0.51	0.54	0.58		23.	48.	
GE Feb19 29	0.87				0.77	0.81	0.85		22.	62.	2
GE Feb19 29.5	1.18				1.11	1.17	1.23		22.	75.	
GE Feb19 30	1.56				1.48	1.80	2.12		35.	73.	7

Figure 2.14: Call options in GE.

Time to Expiration

In general, the further the time to expiration, the greater the need for insurance. The insurance decay slows down, especially for options that are near the money. The longer to expiration, the slower the decay. If you look at delta decay instead of strike decay, the story changes.

I just got done explaining that at the strike level, the further away from ATM, the more linear the decay. However, if I follow option delta decay, how a portfolio that is constantly holding a 0.20 delta option, regardless of what option that is, decays, the story changes. The decay of the 0.20 delta option is in fact exponential. Thus the 0.20 delta option at 2 years will decay more slowly than the 0.20 delta option at 1 year, which will decay much more slowly than the 0.20 delta option at 6 months, and so on.

This means that while you might be used to options decaying a certain way, at 10% out of the money or 20% out of the money, if we follow the decay of options with 0.10 delta at 2 years to expiration and then follow the decay on trading opportunities rolling down to delta, there may be an opportunity to take advantage of theta. Option decay from a delta perspective follows a similar path to ATM options, being short a 0.20 delta option on a constant basis will produce a curve very similar to that of an ATM option.

To sum things up, theta burn following deltas is exponential, but following percentages out of the money is more linear.

Chapter 3
Market Makers, Risk, and the Individual Trader

When I first started trading, I'll admit, as much trading training as I had, I still felt unprepared. It wasn't until I went to work for Scott Kaplan at Quiet Light Trading that I 'got' risk. He used to say to me, "Great trade . . . where is the edge?" He meant this from a capturing dollars perspective and a risk management perspective. Working for Scott taught me not just how to make good trades, but how to capture those dollars.

How Market Makers Make Money

Let's start with a simple concept, a NYSE specialist. If I am a NYSE specialist, I might have a stock XYZ worth $100. As a specialist, I might make the market $99.50 at $100.50, 100 shares 'up' (meaning I am willing to buy or sell 100 shares). If someone moves to buy 100 shares of XYZ, I would take the other side of their buy order and sell them 100 shares at $100.50. Right there I captured .50 in 'edge' or $50.00. However, I have not captured the value, I only have it in theory. In order to gain the value of the edge I need to lock it in via another sell. The only thing I have done has been to sell 100 shares of XYZ at $100.50, which protects the edge for the time being, but does not capture the value. The next step is to capture that value, locking in the edge.

Coming out of my sale, I would like to move my market so that I can potentially capture the 'edge' I sold. My market coming out of that sale might be 100 at 101 up. If someone sells me 100 shares at $100, I have now captured my edge and locked in my profit. However, if someone buys 100 shares from me at $101, what was the end result of my first trade? Was edge captured? No. My bid is now likely $100.50 and my offer is $101.50. If I buy 100 shares for $100.50, despite having two sales of the stock, I only captured edge in the underlying of $50.00. My first trade was done at fair value, and my trade with edge was the $101 sale.

Basically, for the NYSE specialist, if the trade isn't closed, the value isn't captured. You may now understand why tightening spreads caused the demise of many market makers and drove an arrogant man to start a Ponzi scheme (Madoff). Apparently, he had lost the ability to make a living as a market maker, so he began the worst example of using other peoples' money.

Option market making is different. Option market makers must make markets not on just one quote but on hundreds, or in the case of some ETFs and stocks like AAPL, thousands of quotes. How does an option market maker capture edge?

https://doi.org/10.1515/9781501505676-003

Is he or she trying to recreate what a NYSE specialist does on every strike, constantly buying or selling an option then immediately attempting to take the trade off? In some ways yes, but the process of taking off trades is executed in a very different way. While NYSE market makers make markets on price, option market makers make markets around volatility and volatility smile. Ignoring smile for a bit, let's talk about trading around pure volatility.

A standard market maker does not make markets around the options price itself. At the NYSE, a specialist makes the market around fair value, which is uncertain, but is set around where the price of the underlying is trading. For the option market maker, the underlying price is known. The unknown piece is the proper volatility. Thus, the piece of the quote the option market maker is constantly moving around and making markets around is the implied volatility of the option, not the actual price of the option itself. Here is an example:

For an ATM option, the market maker might set the ATM IV at 30 based on how the stock moves historically and on the previous days' trading. For simplicity's sake, the trader might make the market 2 IV points wide (in reality the spread tends to be less than .5% wide). So, he would set the bid at 29% volatility and the offer at 31% volatility. This would set the market on an ATM option in XYZ worth 1.00, based on a 30% volatility (the middle of the market makers vol spread) at .90 at 1.10, or 10 up. If someone buys 10 options for 1.10, that is buying a 31% volatility. In the option market makers pricing model, the value of 1.10 is based on the strike price, time to expiration, price of the underlying, cost of carry, and the forward volatility that just traded. The market maker would then pump IV of the stock up to make the market 30% at 32% volatility, making the option market being quoted 1.00 and 1.20, 10 up (willing to buy 10 for 1.00 and sell 10 at 1.20).

The IV movement seen on a chart like VIX intraday, is a measure of option prices in the SPX. As VIX moves, market makers adjust their markets to the supply and demand of SPX options. When option market makers look at 'vol charts,' they are looking at a 'stock chart' of the volatility of a stock's options. The vol chart, like VIX, just tracks what option market makers are making markets around.

The daily movements of the VIX chart in Figure 3.1 represent the closing prices of how option market makers moved their markets as orders came in to buy or sell.

Figure 3.1: Daily movements of a VIX chart.

Here is the problem that option market makers have that stock market makers don't: They are making markets on a large volume of options. It's not just one option in XYZ, it's many options in XYZ. Thus, the chart above and all volatility that option market makers trade on is made of multiple strikes. Option market makers are making markets on hundreds of quotes at a time per stock, not just a single quote. While this causes multiple layers of complexity, it also allows the option market maker to lock in edge in new ways.

If a market maker is making a 30 vol market in options on XYZ and a trader buys an ATM option at vol of 31, the option market maker may not have to wait for an opposing order on that strike. The edge is already captured. Suppose the trader sells an ATM strike at a 31 vol. The trader might be able to buy the strike that is just out of the money for a 29 or 30 vol level right now. If the option market maker can 'spread' the order, by buying a similar option with similar risk conditions against the trade he or she just made in a short time frame and net 1 extra vol point (buying 30% volatility and selling 31% volatility on strikes right next to each other), the trader may not lock in a pure dollar amount, but the trader may have locked some level of profit. This is how an option market maker captures edge most of the time. The trader buys an option and then sells a similar option at a higher IV relative to the option just purchased. In other words, the market maker is able to buy low and sell high; it is just expressed in terms of implied volatility instead of prices.

Alternatively, the trader may sell an option, then buy a similar option relatively cheaply in comparison. In most cases, the act of *spreading* is the method market makers use to lock in edge in trades made.

Skew

It gets more complicated from there. Because of supply and demand principles, options operate under a concept called *skew* (see Appendix A). Skew represents the relative value of OTM puts and OTM calls relative to ATM options. At a given time, demand for long OTM put options might increase, pushing the cost of OTM puts higher and steepening skew. Alternatively, demand for calls could run hot and skew could flatten. Think of skew as connecting multiple dots together. Based on how trading occurs, the relationship between the dots changes. Another way to look at skew would be to think about an options curve not as a strike or metal bar but as a chain or a rope. If I move links in the chain with my hand, the whole chain will be pushed around, but not uniformly; the same goes for a rope.

Applying this analogy to an options curve, puts get more expensive relative to ATM options or calls get cheaper based on *moneyness*, specifically distance between current price and long-term strike. The ATM options are the center of the spoke; the wings (calls and puts) move in a related but independent way. While OTM options can get steeper relative to ATM, vol must move if there is demand for an option along the curve. Skew is a moving target. However, understanding that IV is mean reverting, the relationship of OTM options and ATM options is also mean reverting and a moving target. One of the values of being an option market maker is making markets on skew. As skew gets out of whack, it allows the option market maker to buy and sell it to traders. Market makers are making markets on skew percentage at the same time they are making markets on volatility, and not just based on flat volatility. They manage the whole curve of options, OTM puts and calls and ATM options.

Think about this complexity: Market makers are trying to manage the level of ATM IV as orders come in, and the level of OTM IV on puts and calls at the same time. Yet managing ATM vol and skew allows for more capturing of edge. If IV is bid and skew is cheap, the market maker can buy OTM options and sell ATM options. If IV is moving around and skew is normal, market makers can spread against other options. If IV is low and skew is high, option market makers can try to buy ATM and sell OTM. There is value for market makers all over the board if they are active and vigilant about what is going on in his or her trades. Using skew and vol together, the trader is able to capture edge when selling a 10, 100, or even 1,000 lot option, as long as the sizing is right. It gets even crazier from there though. For more on puts, calls, skew, and term structure, see Appendix A.

Term Structure

Each option expiration series has its one ATM Implied Volatility (IV). Each option contract within that month will have its own skew. Adding to the complexity is the time to expiration. Every expiration has its own IV value. Like skew and vol, this is a moving target that will change with supply and demand. And like skew and volatility, the spread between months is generally mean reverting. Things such as earnings, a buyout, or a product announcement can throw these out of whack, but even within those events some normalizing takes place.

If market makers see an order in an option for a certain expiration, they can hedge it with an option that has the same expiration or even one that expires on another date. They can hedge it off on another strike in contract month X, but there may be another way to hedge it by buying or selling in a different expiration month. The trading of one month against another is one of the most common ways that market makers lay off risk. If market makers sell one month and buy another at the right *vol spread* they are happy. This is because like skew, the months move together but are also not tied. A buy of one month against another will hedge a large portion of the market maker's risk, but not all of it.

In total, the above amount to one big concept: market makers want to get rid of risk quickly. The use of strike, skew, and term allows them to create positions that have edge up and down. While not necessarily 'locking in' profit, the positions can capture trading edge.

Market Maker Size

The next key to market success is size of the trade. Market makers have a certain amount of risk they are willing to take at any given time. As the ability to make money increases, like any entity looking for risk adjusted returns, the ability of market makers to take the other side depends on how much they can make. This is entirely dependent on edge. Recall that edge is a moving target, but even within that moving target, edge has opportunities to make the market maker money.

If a trader comes in to buy an option, the market maker might start by selling the customer 10 contracts. As the customer begins to buy more options, the market maker may recognize that trading is moving a strike or month out of whack. The more things move out of whack the more the market maker should be willing to sell.

Beyond simple edge is size. Say a market maker's initial market is 29 vol at 31 vol, up by 10. So, the market maker will buy 10 or sell 10 contracts on the currently quoted vols. The next market might be 30 at 32 vol, 10 by 20 (willingness to buy 10 contracts and willingness to sell 20 contracts). The market maker is willing to sell 20 because the price is higher than the first sale, thus it has potentially more edge in the trade. The trader will sell more at a higher price. The goal of the market maker is to slowly increase the size until the current 'fair value' is found, based on supply and demand. If the trader can spread out the risk, even better, given the situation. Imagine demand develops on a certain strike or month. The trader sells 10 in month X and then buys the curve (skew) or another term against it. The trader can sell more the next time the trade comes in. Let's follow the thought process of such a trader:

1. Sell 10 XYZ options, hedge on curve by buying a similar contract along the curve 10 times perhaps a similar strike, but one that is not in as high demand.
2. Sell 20 XYZ options at higher price, hedge in the curve in similar fashion.
3. Sell 50 XYZ options, hedge in another month by buying 50 contracts in a different month.
4. Sell 200 XYZ options, hedge around in other months and the curve as demand for the particular strike hits peak demand.

In the above example, there was demand for one particular options strike. The trader sold more and more of it as the price got higher and higher. Each time the trader sold options he or she used the curve and/or other months to hedge off risk. This allowed the trader to sell options on one strike at higher and higher prices, selling more and more of the option in demand. Once it appears that the buyer of the particular option strike appeared to be finishing, the trader may be willing to be net short options as the trading options push IV to near term extremes. In doing so, the market maker capitalizes on extremely high IV levels caused by demand for the options strike.

In short, trading different months and strikes against one another allows the market maker to capitalize on demand for one option, or one option contract per month. The professional trader should take advantage of this.

The key to the sizing is that the trader needs to always 'be able to trade.' This means that no matter how much 'edge' there is in a trade, not matter how good the trade might seem, the trader always leaves a few 'rounds in the barrel' in order to keep trading. You never know when another customer is going to 'piggy back' a customer trade. Early on in my career I remember thinking that a customer was done with a trade, had found the top, then let it fly only to have another customer walk into the pit and pay more.

Worse yet, if the customer you thought was the top was a smart customer and 'out ahead' of the trade, there could be a swath of orders to follow that trade. The next thing the trader knows, the position is already short thousands of contracts and there are four brokers in the crowd trying to buy. The traders who are able to sit on their hands and not blow their entire inventory on order number one would be able to sell more options at higher prices than those sold early. Those that sold early, in fact may find themselves chasing options on the way up hoping to sell them higher.

If market makers live by the 'always trade the next day' rule, they will never have this happen. Is there 'money left on the table' in a particular trade? Maybe. But over the long haul which trader will make more money? Without a doubt, the trader that holds back. The 'never be unable to trade' rule should carry on beyond the market maker into retail trading.

Market Maker Global Risk

Market makers manage positions on a stock by stock, ETF by ETF, and index by index basis. But they also manage the 'book of trades.' One position might get out of whack but the market maker will likely not go out of business on a large market sell off. This is because the trader manages global risk. On top of monitoring the Greeks of a single position, market makers manage their 'book Greeks.' Market makers make sure they are not carrying too many specific Greeks across the portfolio. The portfolio should not get too short or long gamma, too short or long vega, too short or long delta at any given time. The market maker manages the 'portfolio Greeks,' adding up the amount of delta, gamma, vega, and theta. If one of the portfolio Greeks is too large, the market maker does something about it. A trader may apply the same principles.

The way the trader adjusts positions is by reviewing his or her portfolio. The options that have the least edge in the position are the ones that are taken off. If the trader is short a lot of options in a portfolio, the market maker will review the positions held. The ones that are not 'bid' are the ones that the market maker will move to cover. By buying to close options that don't have a lot of edge, the portfolio has less 'systemic risk.' In a market makers mind, it's one thing to lose because he or she got beat on one position or another. It's another thing for the trader to lose because the portfolio was short a bunch of worthless garbage with no real money in it, that got torched by a selloff in the S&P 500. This is the other piece of being able to trade the next day. Traders must control 'book' risk to ensure that a systemic event, a flash crash, a bank run, you name it, does not put the market maker out of business.

When market makers have traded for several days because option trading is so 'chunky' in that a contract will be extremely popular, they have to manage many positions. As time passes option prices and values change. Options that did have value become near worthless, which changes options for ones that have quantifiable risks to those that are 'units.' One final piece of book risk is 'unit risk.' Market makers, more than anyone, are vulnerable to crazy moves in stocks. Thus, option traders are constantly trying to get out of options worth .05. Options that are worth .05 will pay the market maker over time, but in the near term can cost the trader the house. In trading on their portfolios, market makers may be willing to be net short options (short more options than they are long), but they will never be net short options that are near worthless. Margin risk isn't worth it, and the risk of 'blowing out' will never allow the long-term trader to be short these contracts.

In the coming chapters, we will apply this approach to trading options in a retail portfolio. Hopefully by now, you are already starting to see some of the value of the above.

Chapter 4
Volatility

The most important part of trading options is to understand volatility. More often than not volatility, or 'vol,' is presented as a theoretical concept. If XYZ option does X, then what happens to Y? However, what you need to understand is that volatility is the most important part of recognizing a good trade. If you are able to fully understand the concept of movement (realized vol) and perceived movement (implied vol) you will be able to better distinguish a good trade from bad. In this chapter, I will discuss the zones in which the underlying and options trade. Additionally, I'll talk about how each zone has its own characteristics, levels it trades within, and its general effects on the trader. If you need to brush up on volatility, see Appendix A.

Realized Volatility

The first key to understanding edge is to understand the movement in the underlying. Volatility is mean reverting, not just in how it trades in the long term, but how it trades in the near term. Thus, while long term vol has its mean, current volatility also has levels it will trade within in the near term. The near term can be one week, one month or one year. In order to simplify the process of understanding where volatility is in the near term, at Option Pit we have broken up the levels of current volatility into four main zones. Each zone represents a general level of realized volatility for the overall market for any individual stock. *Zone 1* represents low realized volatility, *zone 2* represents low volatility, *zone 3* is long term mean volatility (remember that long term means tend to be higher than a normal VIX level, because VIX can go super high but has never settled below 8) to elevated volatility, and *zone 4*, high volatility. Each zone has its own characteristics and tendencies. Traders must understand each zone and the signs that the market is moving away from one zone to another.

Zone 1 Ultralow Volatility

One thing traders may easily fail to recognize is how often volatility is ultralow. The VIX has a range from a few occurrences below 10, to many occurrences in the 11s and 12s, to a few in the 60s and 70s. While the long term mean of the VIX might be 18 to 20, there are more occurrences of VIX in the 12s than there are in

https://doi.org/10.1515/9781501505676-004

any other whole number. When VIX is 12, while it is 'ultralow', it is also common and not something that should scare a trader. Ultralow volatility happens for long periods of time and at a much greater rate than 25% of the time. Traders need to be used to these numbers. So, what are the characteristics and ranges of low volatility?

Low volatility is the bottom quartile of realized volatility in a stock; it will have serious dips that can approach a crawling pace of movement. In the S&P 500 this range is going to be realized volatility in the 13% or lower range. It may have small spurts where movement gets toward 15–16% but they will be points not trends. Figure 4.1 is a shot of movement in the SPX in a 4-month time span of 2014. You can clearly see that realized vol is in a tight, low range.

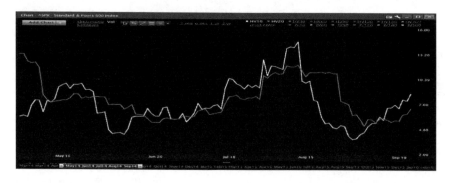

Figure 4.1: Characteristics of Low Realized Vol.

Low vol can be frustrating in that it doesn't mean that every day is low movement. A market can have many days of little volatility intermixed with a dot of high volatility in the form of a single day move of 1–2%. That said, day to day analysis can be boring. When realized vol is low, those who have a plan that involves mass selling of options will probably win. This is because while realized volatility is low, implied volatility, assuming mean reversion, will be higher. For instance, a VIX of 12 usually occurs when realized volatility is between 8 and 10%, *not* when movement is 12. Those traders will have days where they get beaten badly, but they will also get many wins.

These times can be profitable and extremely dangerous, because they can cause traders to think they are smarter than they actually are. This is because when realized volatility is ultralow, option prices tend to be at their most overpriced. If realized volatility is 8 and implied volatility is 12, that is a *huge* premium in relative terms, and that creates a huge edge in points. Even at its peaks in this range, the times when there are 'pops' in movement, options sold at the bottom will be worth just slightly under where the market movement gravitated. Movement increasing from 8 to 12 or 13% has a huge buffer in options built in before the move happened.

Another issue for the trader in this zone is momentum. Volatility assumes that movement is 'regardless of direction.' Yet in low vol times, the market tends to have a direction . . . higher. For those that are not 'dynamically hedging' this can make producing income more difficult. While a *strangle* or *iron condor* is sold at too high a price *regardless of direction* or if the S&P or AAPL decide to move up or down in the same direction, at a slow pace, over and over again, even well-executed condor or strangle trading strategies can get beaten badly. This is because while the volatility sold was at a premium, the pure direction is likely to threaten the short call spread of the condor. The dollar collected selling a condor is going to quickly see the call spread expand to 2 or 3 bucks if you don't monitor and manage the condor's delta. For an overview of spreads and condors, see Chapter 7.

We will discuss IV in zone 1 and then techniques for trading zone 1 shortly, however we first need to understand when zone 1 is ending.

When Does Zone 1 End?

Zone 1 is the most common zone, so how does one recognize its end? The key is seeing the switch in movement. As 'dots' in movement become more common, this zone is ending. If you see an outlier dot once, not a big deal; twice in a 20-day period, not a big deal. It can even happen for a week and not be the end. When the market sees movement for more than a week *or* the market sees a three-standard-deviation move, followed by continued movement in the underlying above the top of zone 1, this *can* be a sign that things are changing. This is especially true if the movement was not driven by a one-off event. However, just be aware that, especially with zone 1, there will be many false signals. If it reverts back for a week or so, that can mean things are retracting back to normal levels. The dollars forgone, assuming that the market is leaving zone 1, relative to the dollars to be made assuming the market will revert back to zone 1's mean, are often not worth it. If you believe that the market is leaving zone 1, even if it takes a month, trading zone 1 like it's zone 2, despite the dollars forgone, will be worth it. A zone 1 trade gone wrong can be costly and take many months to recover if you do not actively manage risk. Zone 1 can create high profit for many months but you may give it all away in one month if you are slow to manage risk. If I am managing a trade to make 0.50 100 times, I am trying to make 5,000. If I let a spread expand to 3.00 before closing, I need to work for six months just to get back to even. This is why zone 1 needs to be aggressively managed.

Zone 2

Zone 2 is the second most common zone. It is what many consider a normal range of realized volatility. This zone is the second quartile in the index or stock's range; in the SPX, this is movement in the 12–17% range. This movement is associated with uncertainty of current market conditions, but awareness of the current conditions that could cause the market to make a large move and volatility to increase. When what is unknown becomes known, that can result in zone 2. One common example is earnings season. During earnings season, there are no stock buybacks, and earnings can be particularly good or bad. Even in a long-term low vol cycle, during earnings season the market tends to enter zone 2. A common market entrant from 2008–2015 was Fed policy; every time changes in Fed policy threatened to occur, the market entered zone 2. We were in zone 2 for a chunk of 2015. See Figure 4.2 for a look at the characteristics of zone 2.

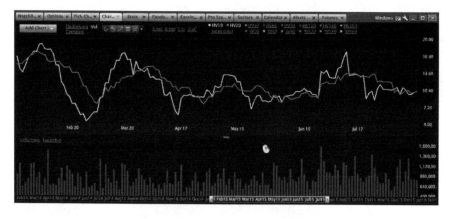

Figure 4.2: Characteristics of zone 2.

Zone 2 can be confusing because it can look so much like zones 1 and 3. When trading in zone 2, short premium trades can be highly effective as zone 2 tends to see volatility revert lower, not higher. A sale in zone 2 when the zone reverts back to zone 1 tends to make a lot of money. However, as the market enters zones away from zone 1, time becomes a factor. Additionally, you should understand that simple trades become trickier in zone 2 because of the potential for volatility to move higher. While most of the time, zone 2 will revert back to zone 1, it is not a sure thing. The times it doesn't and vol moves to zone 3 and 4 (which we will discuss) are when traders can get caught and lose a lot of money if they do not manage risk properly or are to slow to see that volatility is not reverting back to zone 1.

Characteristics of Zone 2

Zone 2 can seem to present real opportunity to the option seller. This is because more often than not the market either stays in zone 2 or heads back to zone 1. However, if it stays in zone 2, there will be a problem for the trader used to trading in zone 1. Zone 2 shows up often, as a top for zone 1 or as a transition to zone 3 or 4. In zone 2, it is key to understand that the strangle or condor may seem expensive, but may actually be cheap given the movement to follow.

One advantage of zone 2 is that momentum becomes less of an issue over weeks of trading as opposed to a move that might occur in the first day or two. However, in zone 2 momentum can cause real pops in volatility and the market can have small moments that seem to be panic. Generally speaking, when vol is in zone 2 it is the price received on the trade that matters and directional price movement in the underlying becomes less of an issue. Yes, the market is moving around much more in zone 2, but the market is moving in one direction.

Zone 2 is quite possibly the best zone for the option seller. However, if you do not prepare for zone 3 or 4, you may set yourself up for an ending worse than the *Sopranos*. Zone 2 is interesting, since it can move to zone 3 or jump to zone 4.

Zone 3

Zone 3 is in many ways like zone 2 in that it represents transition. While zone 3 occurs less often than zone 1 or 2, it is not uncommon. It can happen for a few weeks at a time due to non-US-based risks. Events that can create zone 3 are potentially systemic, but not quite there yet. See December 2014 and January 2015 in Figure 4.3. Note the divergence between the HV10 and HV20 lines, the widest on the chart; this was followed by fast convergence by the end, typical of rapid changes expected to occur during transitions.

Figure 4.3: Characteristics of zone 3.

Zone 3 is a time where vol is high, well above the long-term mean of volatility. It's the point where things can fall off the rails, but . . . often vol just stops before that happens. It can represent levels where things *could* have gone wrong, but didn't. That said, zone 3 represents the market's recognition that there is real fear in the market. This is a time where the market might be really moving 1–1.5% and smaller moves are not the norm. I think the best word to describe this zone is *transition*. It's a level that the market tends to hang around in when it's transitioning from low to high vol or high to low vol. Zone 3 is also the level the market will move toward when there is a threat of a serious issue.

Zone 3 represents truly high vol somewhere above 22% in something like the SPX (as measure by VIX) and below market panic. Zone 3 can be seen most notably in January of 2016 when the VIX held in the 20s for a long time without a true panic sell-off.

Figure 4.4 shows how realized vol can climb continuously. That climbing movement should produce a high VIX. One of the advantages of zone 3 is the huge premiums that can be received relative to where options prices have been in the past. In addition, the tendency of this zone is to head back to zone 2 and even zone 1 relatively quickly. Money can be made trading from the short premium side (selling options), assuming you do a good job of portfolio management (a subject we will delve into). Movement will be higher, but this is often where fear can top out. When that happens, options sales can be juicy as fear in the market is maxed out. IV maintains a huge premium over movement, but when movement dies, IV can completely collapse. Take a quick look at how IV tanked coming out of 'Brexit' in Figure 4.5.

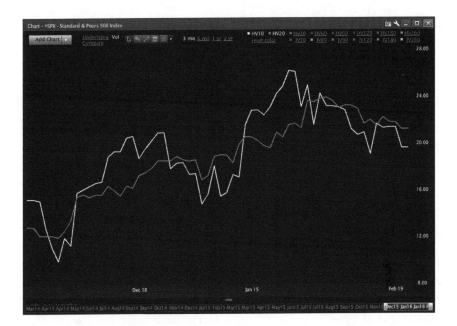

Figure 4.4: HV in the SPX that might occur in zone 3.

Figure 4.5: Movement in the VIX as it moves form zone 3 to zone 2.

In Figure 4.5, VIX fell from over 20 to below 15 in about a week. A massive move.

If you have been a premium seller and you're getting beaten, this can be the level where you are tempted to roll out and increase size because premiums are so juicy. Generally speaking, selling premium wins, unless the market is entering a true volatility event.

However, it is also the time where the market truly spears traders. The market can move from zone 3 to zone 1 multiple times in a short period, as quickly as a week; and you can win nicely on those trades. If you short premium in this zone just once and it moves to zone 4, the trade may blow up. The description of this zone as a transition applies; when it does represent a transition, vol can completely explode, costing you serious dollars in the process.

One final note, if the SPX hits zone 3, it will take a minimum of 6 weeks to see zone 1 again.

Zone 4

This is the panic zone. Zone 4 is the rare air that we seldom see. When we see zone 4, the market is in complete disarray. It can represent a 30% vol if the market has been trading in the low 10s, or more likely into the 40s or 50s if the market is coming from zone 3. This is when the market's worst fears are realized. Lehman Brothers is going bankrupt, or the US is getting downgraded along with Europe having a crisis; most recently China looked like its financial markets were completely melting. You typically don't know zone 4 is happening until you wake up in the morning and futures are down BIG. It typically represents being in zone 3 and seeing an opening gap in the S&P eclipsing 2%. It can lead to a flash crash in today's algorithmic trading. We most recently saw zone 4 (as of the writing of this book) in August of 2015, for example (see Figure 4.6).

The issue with zone 4 is that volatility can go up and up and up. In 2008, the market entered zone 4 in August and did not leave zone 4 until April of the following year. The truth is that while it can seem profitable to sell premium in zone 4, it more often than not loses. This is because vol can keep going for a *long* time. In August 2015 selling premium worked out, it did in 2011 as well; it did *not* in 2008, to the point that it would have more than swallowed the returns made selling in 2011 and 2015 combined. As we state often, the key to vol is to buy high and sell higher.

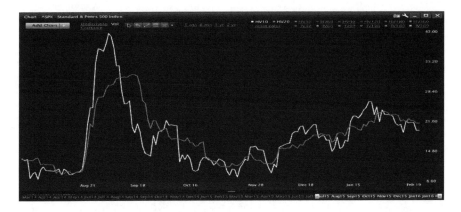

Figure 4.6: Note the zone 4 spike.

So, when is it safe to sell vol in zone 4? When the market hits a new low *after* a vol spike and implied volatility (which we will discuss next) does not spike. Until then, zone 4 is the cash zone, meaning that one should take cash as a position rather than trying to be a hero and attempt to make a fortune. For the more seasoned trader it is a surgical strike zone; there are opportunities to be long vol premium and short vol premium but only in brief stints.

The properly managed portfolio will do well if zone 4 occurs; for the average retail trader, zone 4 typically leads to a major haircut on profits.

Implied Volatility

Implied volatility and realized volatility are very similar. We are going to touch on IV over and over again. For now, we are going to discuss the small differences between the zones when it comes to IV and HV.

The two concepts are sisters. Sometimes realized vol leads implied volatility, other times implied volatility leads realized volatility. Recall that implied volatility is the market's interpretation of what is expected to happen between the day of the trade and the options expiration. It has the same zones as realized volatility, but they can happen at different times and represent different market events. More so than realized vol, implied vol is the market's interpretation of the threats of zone 3 and zone 4 than it is the actual occurrences of those zones. Basically, the fear of underlying movement entering zone 4 can cause zone 3 or 4 to occur in implied volatility terms without zone 3 or 4 type of movement actually happening. Here I'll quickly discuss the zones associated with implied volatility. Zone 1–4 represent the same zones, it's just the causes that change.

Zone 1

Similar to realized vol, zone 1 with implied volatility represents ultra-low volatility and it can stay there for a long time. The main difference is how implied volatility moves in and out of zone 1. Typically zone 1 will be led by implied volatility both in and out. With the S&P 500, zone 1 is below 14 in the VIX. When the market has been moving around, before realized vol measures recognize movement is stopping, implied volatility typically starts to fall. When the market starts to move around, implied volatility will start to move out of zone 1 before the underlying. IV is often described as a leading indicator. IV, especially in indexes, has been described as a lagging indicator. The fact is that it is *both*: IV can lead, as it often does in zone 1, or it can lag as it tends to do once it enters the other zones.

With zone 1, the extremes in implied volatility will be less than the extremes in realized vol. When RV gets to 5, IV might get to 10 or 11%. On the other end, there may be periods where realized vol gets higher quickly, but implied volatility stays somewhat near where it was before the move.

Zone 2

Zone 2 is normal and exhibits standard levels of volatility; it represents a VIX in the 14–18% range. If you look at the occurrences of implied volatility, it will land between 12–16 more often than in any other range, see Figure 4.7.

This is the meat of the market and unlike RV, where zone 1 is possibly the most common zone, in implied volatility, zone 2 is going to be the most common area in which the options market hangs. Implied volatility in zone 2 tends to be above RV and, when movement increases, zone 2 is where implied volatility is most likely to be slow to react. Within zone 2 the market typically acts normally. The S&P 500 will be generally rallying, there may be blips of volatility, but the market is moving higher. Zone 2 will have the bull market highs in volatility. When there is a Fed meeting, the high end of Zone 2 is likely to be reached. Zone 2 is where the market moves ahead of non-farm payroll reports. Within individual equities, there may be some earnings reports, especially in lower vol stocks. To learn zone 2, follow the VIX during the bulk of 2012 and 2014.

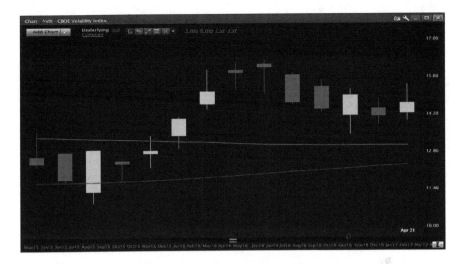

Figure 4.7: Zone 2 as seen in the VIX.

What makes zone 2 different is that unlike realized volatility which can hang in zone 1 for a long time, even when realized volatility is in zone 1, implied can hang at the low end of zone 2 rather than dipping into zone 1. It takes an extremely long period of time to pull IV into zone 1. Thus, even if realized volatility is 8, 9, or 10%, implied volatility might stay above 14%. When IV is in this bottom range of zone 2 it can stay there for a longer period of time even if RV starts to move. And once IV moves within zone 2 it tends to stay in zone 2 for too long and then quickly move back.

Traders should plan to do the bulk of their trading within this IV zone 2 and then expect to see RV in zone 1 *and* zone 2. However, be aware that zone 2 in both realized and implied vol invites a recency bias, the belief that things will go back from whence they came. Traders that trade zone 2 think IV is going to be in this zone forever; it won't.

Zone 3

Zone 3 represents elevated volatility in the VIX, generally at 18–23, but can be as high as 28 or 30. Zone 3 is when the market goes through a short period of fear but has not hit the panic zone. Zone 3 occurs less often than zone 1 and zone 2, but it can happen quickly. Typically, unlike zone 1 and 2, it happens simultaneously with market movement. When the market starts having multiple 1% daily moves, it is getting into zone 3, and IV will quickly catch up to RV. IV can spike into zone 3 with movement of the underlying (realized volatility) meeting it, most notably the fiscal cliff in 2012. In 2012, IV got to 28% in the VIX and movement never came close. Zone 3 can be scary, but presents some high IV that can give you a chance to sell market premium, if you are positioned properly. On the other hand, when IVs get to zone 3 they can expand . . . for a long time.

Zone 3 in RV is somewhat rare in a *bull market*; however, it does happen in short spurts. It happened in 2012 ahead of the fiscal cliff, and it happened during 2014 a few times. In a *bear market*, zone 3 becomes much more common. The SPX will spend months in zone 3 with blips of zone 4. The good news is that you can see zone 4 coming in a zone 3 situation in a bear market. Looking at bull and bear, zone 3 is when markets tend to transition to serious volatility.

In zone 3, be prepared to sell premium, but be prepared to hedge and to leave money on the table. Traders willing to trade small and opportunistically will be able to make many small trades for short periods of time that make more than what you might make in zones 1 and 2. Quickly touching on sizing, this zone invites smaller size and more traders for shorter periods of time.

Zone 4

Just like zone 4 in realized volatility (RV), this is the market in total panic and represents true fear in the market. The VIX is typically above 30, although zone 4 could be lower than that level. Like zone 3, the market is moving. However, unlike zone 3, zone 4 is almost always reactionary. IV pops into zone 4 because the market popped into zone 4. As rare as it happens, zone 4 is the level you need to be prepared for. Your approach to trades should flip; when it comes to vol, sell low and buy lower and vice versa. Its more than true with IV.

The main difference between RV and IV in zone 4 is that IV tends to be a little slower to calm down. Yet, zone 4 has a lot of pump fakes; in 2011 the market went to zone 4 in August for a few weeks, calmed down, and then showed its face again in October. In zone 4, you should be short and sweet and on the attack. The slow play is not in effect and standard 'income' trades should be dropped because they will likely get caught. This means that of you have a 'system' to sell Iron Condors, Butterflies, or other short premium trades, you also need to see what's in front of you and *not* blindly trade your system. The standard trades most traders rely on are *not* what you should be trading in zone 4. You need to be ready to trade for an hour or a day, *not* all day for three weeks through systematic short premium trades.

Zone 4 is, in short, almost exactly the same as zone 4 in the RV section because the two are so similar, but without the duration. You should be willing to execute short trades in zone 4 and close them when the market threatens zone 3. More importantly, you should be willing to flip your approach to trading and buy premium or set up hedges in zone 4. We will spend a chapter discussing hedging and how to trade in zone 4 in later chapters.

Chapter 5
What Is Edge?

Edge is the value created in an option's sale or purchase when you are able to exploit fair value to produce consistent profits. There are those that teach that edge is the embedded 'extra premium' that naturally exists in selling options. This is the foundational thesis of my first book, *The Option Trader's Hedge Fund*. In this book, I introduced the concept of TOMIC (The One Man Insurance Company). This is an approach to trading options based on market volatility and discipline, a technique similar to that used for risk assessment by insurance companies. In this chapter, we begin to break that concept apart by discussing the relative value of an option, and how to determine if an option should be bought or sold. Thus, edge is not just the 'insurance' value of an option; edge is the value created when you can buy an option cheaply relative to normal levels, or sell an option at a higher than normal rate. For instance, if you have a value of 1.00 on an option and the market maker acquires edge from a bid-ask spread, the trader that is initiating the order wants to buy it for *any* number less than 1.00. You may find a period of time where IV is so depressed that the 1.00 option is offered at a buy of 0.95 or a sale of 1.05. The question many traders have when evaluating option pricing is how to tell a good trade from a bad trade. It's time to delve into the relative value of an option, how traders develop the true value of an option, and how to determine what should be bought and what should be sold.

Edge

What is edge, really? Edge, in short, is exploiting option pricing to take advantage of overly cheap or expensive contracts. In capturing edge, traders need to be able to sell premium when IV is high and buy premium when IV is low, but how do you recognize this? It starts with knowing the volatility of the product under consideration. SPX traders that stand in the pit all day generally *know* the volatility. One of my true mentors of trading, as I mentioned in Chapter 3, was the Gator, Scott Kaplan. In the products he traded, he knew volatility levels so well that he could walk away from the pit or the trading screen for a week, and if I named the volatility levels and the current level of the S&P he could walk into the pit and start trading. Thus, when he was in the pit, watching trading all day, he could spot the good ones from the bad in an instant.

I am not expecting all the readers of this book to understand volatility at the level of a professional trader, however, you can prepare to trade like a professional.

https://doi.org/10.1515/9781501505676-005

Additionally, the ability to initiate a trade gives you the ability to skip the 'average trades' and go after the trades that are clear winners. The key is volatility charts. Yes, every trader should have a list of stocks they follow closely. But because of the availability of good vol charts and the trader's understanding of the zones, you should be able to figure out where IVs of a trade are within a few minutes. The steps are simple:

1. Review the HV of the underlying at the 10, 20, and 60 day levels.
2. Review the IV of the product.
3. Establish the product's trading zones for HV and IV based on bullets 1 and 2. In what zone is the product's HV and IV trading?
4. Know the zone of the whole market.
5. Determine if there is a trade with edge.

Let's walk through this trading process.

Like the market as a whole, each stock has its own levels of realized volatility and implied volatility it hangs in. The product will typically reach levels that are at the extremes but it does not stay there for long, and will have normal levels in which it meanders—between zones 1 and zone 4. Let's take a look at a chart of movement in AAPL from September 2015 to September 2016 at the 10, 20 and 60 day HV levels.

10 Day HV

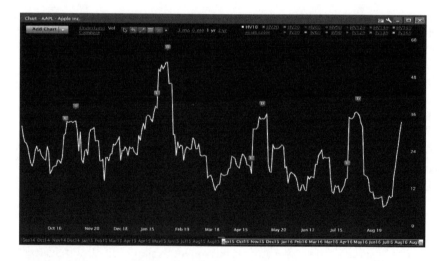

Figure 5.1: 10 day HV of AAPL over the period of a year.

As one can see in Figure 5.1, 10 day HV (10HV) has its ranges; at its absolute extremes, it can get near 50 as it did in January 2016 (we'll discuss why that was the case in a little bit). Looking at HV10, I would put zone 1 around 17% HV or lower. I would put anything above 35 in zone 4. Zones 2 and 3 are a little more difficult. You might eyeball zone 3 above 26 and zone 2 between 17 and 26 (zone 2 should normally be the biggest zone).

20 Day HV

In the 20 day HV graph in Figure 5.2, the same holds true, although the zones represent different levels in 20 day HV. This is less representative of near-term realized vol and more of how much the underlying moved on a relatively smooth basis. You can see the levels of 20 day HV are: zone 1 below 16, zone 2 from 16 to 23, zone 3 from 23 to 30 and zone 4 at 30 or higher.

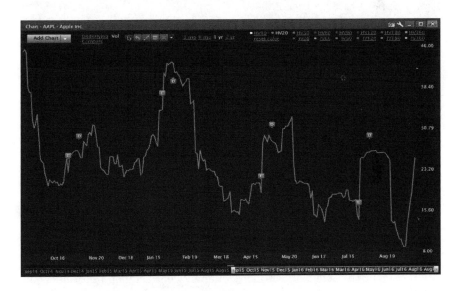

Figure 5.2: Apple 20 day HV for the same period.

60 Day HV

60 day HV will still having some similarities to the zones of the market and to the zones of the underlying. However, it should show down the trends. In this case,

AAPL HV was trending lower *but,* since mid-August, it had ticked up significantly after bottoming out. Longer term HV is a great tool to help traders to recognize whether a pop in 10 day or 20 day HV is just a blip, or the real thing. In this case, it appeared the move was in fact a real thing. The zone of the 60 day HV in Figure 5.3, which should reflect the near term mean for 10 and 20, appeared to be about 26%. Therefore, if the 10 day HV was above 26%, that had to be zone 3 or 4, and below that was probably zone 1 and 2.

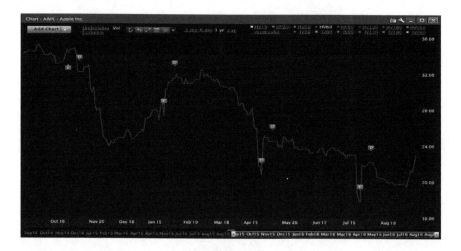

Figure 5.3: 60 day HV for AAPL for the same period.

Review the IV of the Product

Unlike HV, which should have many iterations that traders look at, IV has fewer durations to study but with more dimensions. Durations are the days to expiration of the contract from which IV can be derived, typically one month, two months, or three months. Dimensions are all of the different variants of IV in a contract month, different strikes along different contract months, or how puts and calls trade in the different durations relative to ATM IV or how far OTM options trade relative to nearer the money OTM options. Additionally, dimensions represent the relationships of one expiration duration to another. IVs are in many ways four dimensional, ATM, above the money, below the money, far out of the money on both ends, and with different expiration months.

Traders reading this book, for the most part, really only need to pay attention to one duration, maybe two. However, they also need to know what skew and term structure look like (thus, in many ways they look at lots of durations). Before worrying about skew and term structure, the first step is to figure out what is high and low 30 day IV (IV30). From 30 day IV, every other piece of volatility is derived. It's the duration that is most active, it's the place that every trader looks to evaluate premium, and it is the duration that is most fairly priced. In viewing IV30 and getting an accurate representation of where implied volatility with a duration of 30 days to expiration is, you can formulate any trade and have a reasonable chance at creating edge. IV30 is so important that you could skip skew and term structure and still create trades with edge. (By the way, *don't skip skew and term structure.* Just because you can, doesn't mean you should; there is far more edge to be found by examining all three).

IV30

We are going to use Livevol for AAPL data in our 30 day IV examples; however, many other brokerage platforms also put out IVs. In addition, for those that want to use an extremely discounted broker, the CBOE puts out a host of indexes based on VIX that give an accurate view of 30 day IV. For instance, while we are going to use Livevol's IV30 for AAPL, CBOE publishes VXAPL which is the VIX of AAPL options with 30 days to expire. Let's take a look at two years of 30 day IV for AAPL is shown in Figure 5.4.

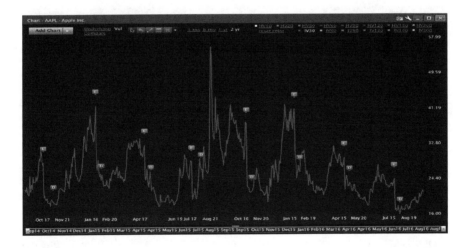

Figure 5.4: Two years of 30 day IV for AAPL.

While you can see that there are highs and lows, 30 day IV seems to have a level it centers around, even more than HV10, 20, and 60. In this case, I would put it between 23 and 26 based on the IV levels to which AAPL tends to gravitate. Outside of that, you can see stress levels and extremes. Reviewing these extremes and knowing when earnings are coming, you can set up many trades. Thus, in reviewing the above, at the time we were evaluating, you can see that 30 day IV was coming off a two-year low, but rising. The next move in the IV appears to be higher, not lower. From here, you can set up a trade somewhat easily without looking at any other pieces of vol. However, you would be trading on only a partial story.

Term Structure

In reviewing the above, you might think, "I want to buy options." You can do many trades; but without looking at term structure, how the contract months are priced against one another, you can't develop the best way of knowing what to buy and, if so inclined, what to sell. Let's take a quick look at AAPL term structure from Livevol. The below represents the aggregate vol in each contract for AAPL. In short, if you were to run an aggregate vol in the month of October, the vol would be 21.35%. If you were to run the same aggregate in November the IV for AAPL options in that month would be 25.33%.

Sep23(W)	Sep30(W)	Oct07(W)	Oct14(W)	Oct21	Oct28(W)	Nov18	Dec16	Jan20'17	Feb17'17	Mar17'17
22.97	21.96	21.17	20.87	21.35	25.59	25.33	23.88	23.21	24.68	24.22
-2.63	-1.48	-1.05	-0.73	-0.63	-0.77	0.00	0.09	0.13	-0.20	-0.13

Figure 5.5: The aggregate vol in each contract for AAPL.

Looking at the above, you can see that if you were looking to buy options in the near term, the October 14 or regular October contract might make sense because relative to the rest of the contracts, they are low-priced. Additionally, aggregate IV for October 14 and 21 were lower than the months in front *and* the months behind those contracts. If you want to own a longer-term contract, you might look at January 2017, since IV was cheaper in January than it was in December and November. Alternatively, if you are looking to sell options without explosive gamma against a long, you could sell the September 30 or the October 7 contract for a nearer-term trade. Longer term against a January trade, you could sell November or December *because* they were more expensive. The point is that while you might want to own premium, without looking at the term structure you can't pick the best spots to trade.

Skew

Skew is the relative price of OTM puts and OTM calls when compared to ATM implied volatility. Typically, in equities, calls will have lower IV than ATM options and puts will have higher IV. However, the IVs of puts and calls relative to ATM options moves constantly. Thus, skew as a whole can become expensive or cheap. There are times where puts, regardless of strike, are expensive and at other times calls can be as well. Calls and puts tend to move freely from each other as the option flow (customer orders) tend to be unrelated to each other. By having an idea of how expensive puts and calls should be, and where skew normally trades, you can figure out trades that make sense. This is *especially* true in the indexes where there is less put selling on a relative basis.

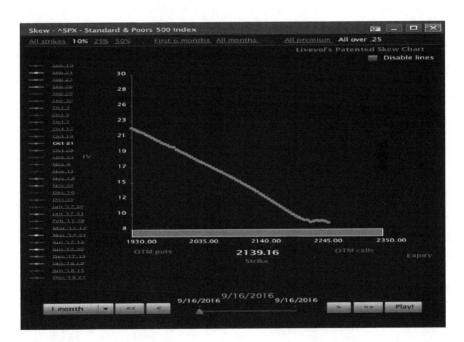

Figure 5.6: A steep skew curve.

When skew is steep as in Figure 5.6, trades may be extremely favorable, and when skew is flat, trades may also be favorable. However, trades that work in one condition tend not to work in the other. When skew is normalized and you don't see an overall advantage to being long or short one side of the curve (skew as a whole is not out of 'whack'), skew can help in strike selection because it will help the trader see which strikes may be mispriced even if the curve is mostly normal. Strikes can be out of whack even if the curve as a whole is not.

If you aren't trading skew, you can still use it to your advantage, especially in equities, as one strike can get overbought or oversold. By looking at the curve, you may be able to pinpoint opportunity between strikes. Strikes as close as one price increment might offer an advantage over another. You can figure this out by looking at the curve within one month. This is *especially* true in equities where one customer can push things around. If customers want to own a call or put, they can move volatility by insisting on buying that strike; the other strikes around that option will not move nearly as quickly and may produce an opportunity. This is, as we explained in Chapter 3, because the nature of market makers is to not want a position. Because they are trying to adjust for customer order flow, if a large customer continuously buys or sells a strike or contract month, that customer's order flow will move volatility. This action we used to call 'pushing vol around' when on the floor. Even in some of the most liquid equities this can be true. Figure 5.7 presents a snapshot of AAPL Skew.

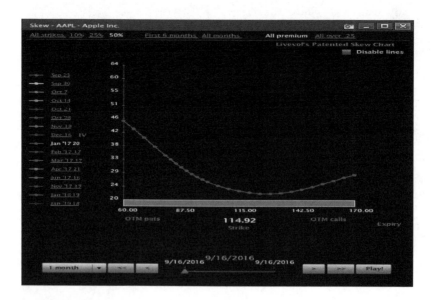

Figure 5.7: AAPL skew.

Within equities, skew can get out of whack, but it is subtle at times. It almost always develops if customers are buying or selling strikes. Take a look at the skew chart in Figure 5.7. The 105 strike in Figure 5.7 ever so slightly appears to be overpriced relative to the 100s and 110s. On the bullish side, the 125s are the cheapest option on the board. Considering that these are options with 3 months to expire, you could formulate a trade using these options as a base. Alternatively, if you want to sell an option, those two are not the strikes to select. Something as simple as avoiding a bad sale or making a good buy can make a huge difference in the result of a trade.

Know the *Zone* of the Market

As we discussed in the previous chapter, the market as a whole has zones; this applies to any product. Whether you are looking at cornmeal, mash, or oil options, you still need to know what the root vol looks like in the product. This is because there is always a dog and always a tail when it comes to volatility. If you want to dig down a rabbit hole, you could say, "This market affects the next market, and the next market affects another," and so on. However, I can tell you, professionals are aware of what is going on around them, but until something bleeds into what they are trading, they only look at the main dog of the product. For the average traders this makes sense as well. Until volatility 'bleeds' into the market they are trading, it makes little sense to get overly concerned about inter-market volatility. This doesn't mean ignoring macro events; it means not allowing IV decisions to be affected until the volatility actually starts to move.

When trading equities, there is really only one dog, the S&P 500; you might argue in some small companies it's the Russell 2000 or the NDX in the case of some technology stocks. However, in the end, all stocks are driven by movement in the S&P 500. If you know the zone of the VIX, you know the zone of the SPX. For equities, if you know the zone of the SPX, you know the zone of the market. Every volatility in every ETF and stock has volatility correlated to the S&P 500 save a few commodity ETFs and possibly the most defensive stocks. In the most extreme times, even uncorrelated ETFs and defensive stocks will have volatilities that start to correlate with the VIX. Take a look at Figure 5.8, where the vols of a few unrelated ETFs move with vol of SPY.

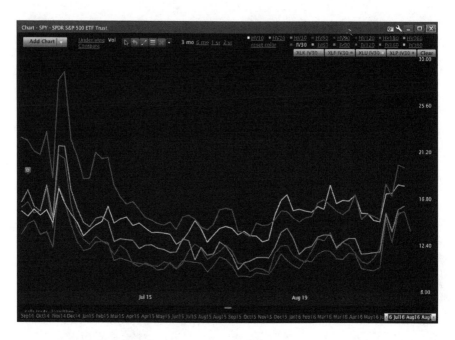

Figure 5.8: IVs of several Sector ETFs of the S&P 500 from top to bottom XLF, XLU, XLK, XLP, and SPY.

In Figure 5.8, you can see that while the volatilities don't move in lock step with SPY, you should easily be able to see that if the above indexes are not tied, they are clearly connected with the individual ETFs being higher than SPY, but moving with the index nonetheless. The point is that the zone of an ETF or stock as a relative level is determined by the overall market. In short, you cannot determine the zone of IV of an equity or ETF without first knowing the IV of SPY.

Looking at individual equities, going back to our charts of AAPL HV, Figure 5.9 shows that when the market was in zone 3, as it was in January of 2016, AAPL hit its zone 4. The same holds true for June of 2016.

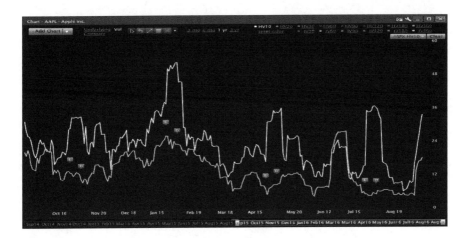

Figure 5.9: HV10 of AAPL relative to HV10 of the S&P 500.

The same holds true for every other HV chart.

Select the Trade

Now that the trader has established the zone of the market and has a strong understanding of the direction of HV—is it going up, down, or sideways—you can make a decision on stock movement. Now that you have looked at IV level and the IV of the overall market, you can determine what option trade fits the current expected realized vol. You can figure out whether trade conditions exist because of the equity market as a whole, or because there is an edge with the specific trade. It is important to *never* get lost in a stock or ETF. The market drives everything in crisis. It's the rest of the time that edge can be found. Skills in evaluating realized vol, implied vol facets, and the overall market will enhance your trading skills. Without that skill, traders are unlikely to succeed. In the next chapter, we will begin to put the rubber to the road in showing you how to evaluate when to enter many trades that can be profitable . . . given the right circumstances.

Chapter 6
Locking in Edge

We just spent the last chapter explaining how to spot edge. However, given the market, edge in a trade can account for nothing. A trade is not a winner until the value is locked in. In this chapter, we will talk edge and locking in trades.

When I started trading, Scott Kaplan, my trading mentor, asked me, "Where is the edge?" What he meant was: Is there a way to lock and/or protect that value? Because if the value of a trade isn't locked in, the trade might not hold value. If the trade doesn't hold value, it doesn't have edge. Thus, the only way to trade with edge is to buy something against a sale or to sell something against a buy. Let me give you an example from a market maker's perspective.

When I was a floor trader, I made markets in ETF trading as EEM, the iShares MSCI Emerging Markets Index. At one point near the close, a broker came in looking to buy a near-term strangle, as I recall the strangle had about 60 days to expire. What made the strangle so interesting was that I had it worth about 0.10 less than what the broker was willing to pay. The set-up was great and on its surface the strangle looked like a winner. However, it was late in the day, and you never know when customers will pay because they think the stock is about to move. Basically, a strangle with 0.10 in it looks great until the next day when the underlying moves dramatically (something that happens if the trade is left alone). Therefore, on its own, I would have done this trade in small size. However, if I could 'lock in the value' I wanted as much of this trade as possible. (For more information on strangles and other spreads mentioned in this chapter, see Chapter 7).

Here is how I 'locked it in': Another broker, at the exact same time, was trying to sell a call tied to the stock that had about a 90-day duration, while at the same time that one broker was trying to buy the strangle, I had an option to sell. The option sale (by the customer to me), was just a touch better than fair value. I had about a penny or two of edge in the trade.

On its own, I would have never bought the calls, but with the strangle available, that trade went from marginal to crucial to me making money. I called broker B, asked if he still had his calls to sell, and bought 1,000 contracts. Once I had secured a purchase of the calls, I sold the other broker 750 of the strangles. Using one broker's trade against another, I managed to lock in value in the trade. I was long, what amounted to a cheap longer-term straddle (calls plus short stock sold at delta neutral, creating a synthetic straddle). This combined long calls with long synthetic puts, along with long calls and long stock, against a short near-term

https://doi.org/10.1515/9781501505676-006

strangle. With the whole thing at delta neutral, the trade amounted to a long calendar spread for 0.07 (0.05 in each option from the strangle and 0.02 in the calls). Even market makers do not expect that kind of value in a calendar spread, which priced on its own, might have 0.03 in it.

You may wonder how I determined the right number of contracts I needed to offset the trade, and how I knew that the two would 'lock in' value. The answer lies in dynamic vega management. In Chapter 12, we will dig into dynamic vega and how to quantify offsetting spreads. I used these techniques to piece together the trade. For now, think of the edge I captured as more than twice what I would normally get from two different brokers. Knowing that this wasn't one customer with an agenda, but two customers with offsetting agendas, made me more confident in the trade. If I saw a calendar with 0.07 I might try to do 200, but because I pieced this together, I could do more, knowing that it wasn't a trader that was too "smart" (a trader that knows something I don't).

The Retail Trader

The retail trader does not have the advantage of having the ability to trade directly with brokers to generate offsetting trades like the one above. However, the power to initiate trades means that the retail trader can create their own edge. The key is finding edge via the spread trade.

As a retail trader, you must accept that one leg of the trade will be executed at a fair value price. However, if the other leg of the trade is too cheap or overpriced, you should not mind executing it because *any* edge to a retail trader is a win. The key is to follow the right steps:
1. Establish the option you *want* to trade
2. Establish the offsetting contract that is the cheapest to hedge the trade
3. Execute the hard side of the trade
4. Execute the easy side of the trade
5. Manage the position
6. Exit or hold to expiration

Establish the Option You *Want* to Execute

This is an option that is typically over- or underpriced. Its pricing is often driven by a large block order, or a group of large block orders. Institutions hedging or speculating typically have enough information in their decision tree that moving IVs by a point is not going to affect their decision. Paying 0.05 over fair value is the cost of business when you want exposure to the underlying, equaling 5 million shares of stock. However, one thing many retail traders do not know is that when a large trade pushes markets out of whack, market makers keep things that way until someone notices, then the market maker trades the minimum they can to move things back in line and avoid giving up edge. The average retail or *prop trader* (a proprietary trader who trades their own assets), is going to trade fewer than 100 contracts at a time. This is too small to move things for most market makers. Prop traders set up their trades to take advantage of being small and are prepared to trade inexpensive options.

Establish the Offsetting Contract

Before executing the trade that has edge, make sure that it actually *has* edge. How is this done? By quickly finding an option to buy or sell, you reduce the risk of the edge trade dramatically. This can be a calendar spread if term structure is off; this can be a credit, debit, or butterfly spread if there is a long strike out of whack. In determining the option to buy, one must spend the time to evaluate the curve (skew) and term structure. If going with term structure, make sure that overall IV matches with the trade. In determining a spread within the same contract month, the vol curve is key. We will dig into setting up these spreads on an individual basis in an upcoming chapter. The key is to be aware that in order for a trade to actually be a good trade, there *must* be something to buy or sell at the wrong price, and, on the other side of the trade, that the same thing is bought or sold at a fair price at a minimum (or in a perfect world, at a price that is too high or low depending on what you are hedging, so that you could make money on both sides of the trade).

The Hard and Soft Side of a Trade

Just because a contract is out of whack doesn't mean it's easy to buy or sell. When a strike or contract month is thrown out of whack, it won't necessarily be easy to trade. That all depends on the order flow (customer orders). If strike was thrown out of whack by one large trade, what is done might be done and it likely will be ignored by order flow; an offer could sit there and never trade. Market makers are not stupid and will not simply execute the trade that you want at the current mid-price. They will only fill it if they think they will be able to trade something against it. This is especially true if the trade was put up as a cross or facilitated by a firm (a cross is when a broker finds both sides of a trade and meets prices in the middle). Facilitating a trade means the brokerage firm takes down the whole trade and the customer pays a high commission.

Let's take a look at how a big trade in SCHW can be traded in the market:

Time	Root	Option	Qty ▼	Price	Exchange	Condition	Market	IV	Underlying
2:44	SCHW	Dec16 30 C	20000	1.80	MIAX	PriceVariation	1.80 x 1.90	28.00	30.47
2:45	SCHW	Dec16 30 C	9047	1.80	MIAX	PriceVariation	1.80 x 1.90	28.00	30.47

A firm clearly was out to sell the December 30 calls as 20,000 of them were sold (the equivalent of 2,000,000 shares); this trade moved vol pretty hard. If you wanted to trade off of the order flow above, you could repeat the trade above. In setting up a trade, you might sit back on the bid on the December 30 calls and then go after the December 31 calls or the December 29 calls, depending on the direction of the underlying.

Another scenario occurs if there is a term or strike on the asset that is being actively 'swept' by the market (chased by customer order flow). In this case, multiple traders or one large trader is aggressively attacking a strike or term. In the example below, RR Donnelley trades met this description. The December 18 calls were aggressively purchased with the trader paying up to 0.30 on a market that started out at 0.15–0.20 and traded as low as 0.15 and up to 0.30. The point is that someone, or *more than one*, wanted to own the December 18s. There is no rush to own these as it will not be difficult to fill a sale in this case if you are looking to sell the 18s at 0.25.

Today's largest trades									
Time	Root	Option	Qty ▼	Price	Exchange	Condition	Market	IV	Underlying
11:55	RRD	Dec16 18 C	576	0.25	ISE	IntermarketSweep	0.15 x 0.25	29.00	16.19
10:10	RRD	Dec16 18 C	434	0.15	CBOE	Regular	0.15 x 0.20	23.00	16.20
10:10	RRD	Dec16 18 C	307	0.15	BATS	IntermarketSweep	0.15 x 0.20	24.00	16.20
2:29	RRD	Dec16 18 C	300	0.30	BATS	IntermarketSweep	0.20 x 0.35	30.00	16.22
12:15	RRD	Dec16 18 C	162	0.30	CBOE	PriceVariation	0.25 x 0.30	30.00	16.21
11:55	RRD	Dec16 18 C	143	0.25	PHLX	IntermarketSweep	0.15 x 0.25	29.00	16.19
11:55	RRD	Dec16 18 C	129	0.25	CBOE	IntermarketSweep	0.20 x 0.25	29.00	16.19
11:55	RRD	Dec16 18 C	120	0.25	MIAX	Regular	0.15 x 0.25	29.00	16.16
11:55	RRD	Dec16 18 C	113	0.25	MIAX	Regular	0.15 x 0.25	29.00	16.16
3:39	RRD	Oct21 17 C	100	0.25	ARCA	AutoExecution	0.20 x 0.25	27.00	16.39
12:14	RRD	Dec16 18 C	100	0.30	BOX	AutoExecution	0.30 x 0.35	29.00	16.23
12:10	RRD	Dec16 18 C	100	0.30	AMEX	AutoExecution	0.25 x 0.30	30.00	16.28
2:19	RRD	Dec16 18 C	99	0.30	BATS	IntermarketSweep	0.20 x 0.30	30.00	16.24
12:14	RRD	Dec16 18 C	90	0.30	BATS	IntermarketSweep	0.30 x 0.35	29.00	16.24
11:55	RRD	Dec16 18 C	87	0.25	NASDAQ	AutoExecution	0.15 x 0.25	29.00	16.19

Figure 6.1: Shows large orders in RRD that traded on a specific day.

The key is to understand what is harder to fill and what is easier to fill. When edge is created by one block trader, expect that there will *not* be a lot of follow-up.

Traders in this case should work to execute the side of the trade that has edge to it first. Thus, in this case, the hard side of the trade was executing the option with edge. After the option with edge is filled, *then* you should execute the hedge. The worst case in this scenario is usually a trade executed for fair value (if you can't fill the hedge).

Alternatively, when there are lot of sweepers and it is not hard to sell a strike or contract month, traders should assume that getting filled on the side of the trade with edge will be easy. The hedge on the other hand, with market makers knowing there are many contracts to be laid off, will not be as easy to fill. In this case, execute the hedge, then let the trade with edge come to you. Again, going with this route, the worst the trader will end up with is fair value, and more likely with edge as an order will come along eventually. When a spread with edge is being set up where the hard side of the trade is the hedge, it is much more likely to end up having edge than the other way around. Use speed to get a hedge in this scenario, then be patient in letting a trade come to you. More often than not, these spreads will produce.

Execute, Manage, Exit

Once a trade can be made, execute the hard side to fill and *then* the easy side to execute the trade with edge. Stick to the plan of the trade. If the trade does not have value, does not have edge, don't execute the trade. Assuming the trade is done properly, it should be managed professionally. While we are going to spend lots of time discussing how to manage trades, I want this to be a clear point, we are going to hit on this many times: edge *matters*. If you put on a trade that you believe has edge, and that is proven to be incorrect, you should kill the trade by closing it quickly. If a trade is executed with edge and the assumptions change, kill the trade. Alternatively, if the trade is great and makes quick money, more than you were expecting, kill the trade. The point is, if the trade goes as unexpected, win or lose, get out. Finally, if the trade hits an *adjustment point* (which we will discuss in later chapters), make the adjustment. If the trade gets away, kill the trade. If the trade wins, kill the trade and take the money. Adjusting and managing are huge pieces of success, but they are determined by the edge in the trade. If the edge changes, take the money or take the licks. Take the time to be aware of how your position is changing and how you lose or make money. We are about to dig into each trade and then put a portfolio together in coming chapters.

Part II: **Using Spreads**

Chapter 7
A Quick Review of Spreads

Throughout this book, I discuss how to evaluate different trades in the market given specific market conditions. While this book assumes that the reader has knowledge of most spreads, I think it is worth the time to describe each type of complex spread. In this chapter, I'll briefly discuss what makes each spread, what makes each spread make money, and the goals of the trade at onset.

The Call Spread

A *call spread* is very similar to a long call. The construction of the long call spread is pretty simple, but offers two possibilities. A call spread can be done for a debit or a credit. The debit version involves buying a call close to the underlying price, usually at or slightly out of the money, although it can be executed in the money as well. We will walk through the most common version which is a debit spread with a long call slightly out of the money.

In executing the *call debit spread*, the trader is looking for movement, but is more interested in actual movement than the market thinking movement might increase in the future. Thus, it is more of a 'gamma-centric' trade than 'vega-centric' trade. The construction involves buying a call slightly OTM and then selling a call that is further OTM. In the example below, the SPX was trading 2355; the trader opened an April 2375–2400 call spread, buying the 2375 calls for 6.50 and selling the 2400 calls for 1.35. Figure 7.1 shows a P&L chart.

Notice the trade is heavy on delta and gamma, and relatively light on vega for an index trading at 2350. The advantage of the trade is that cost is limited and profit potential is big. As these spreads go further out in time, the trader gives up some cost; the spread is more expensive in exchange for more time. The trader hopes that the underlying will rally, in which case the trader makes money. The goal of the trade is for the underlying to *do* something, in this case, to move higher.

The *credit spread* is just the opposite. The trader sells a call out of the money and buys a call further out of the money. Like the debit spread, this can be done at and in the money. In the case of a trade above, a trader does the opposite of the debit spread.

https://doi.org/10.1515/9781501505676-007

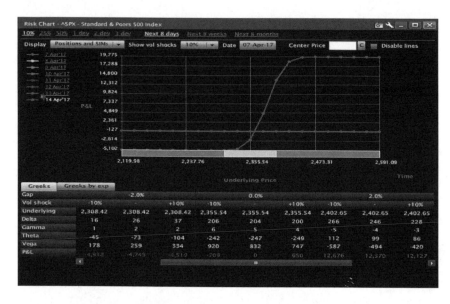

Figure 7.1: The payout of a call spread near expiration.

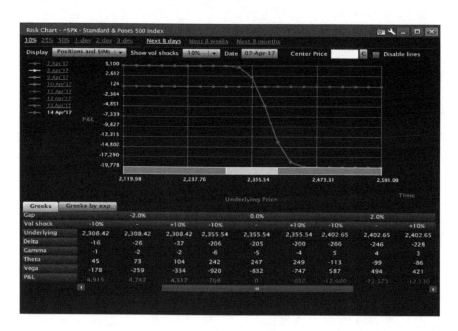

Figure 7.2: The payout of a short call spread near expiration.

In this case, the trader believes the underlying will not rally above 2375. If it does, the trader loses; if it does not rally, the trader keeps the value of the spread, in this case a touch over 5.00. The goal of this spread is for the underlying to *not* rally and/or rally slowly settling below 2375. Both of these spreads can be great, but they need to be formed on an opinion—will the underlying move or will it not move?

The Put Spread

A put spread long or short (debit or credit) has the same goals as a call spread— just in the opposite direction. The debit holder hopes the underlying will drop. In comparing the two, you want to see a rally in the case of a debit spread, while with a credit spread you hope the underlying will rally.

A long put spread tends to be short delta and long vega. However, like the long call spread, it seeks movement more than it wants a pop in volatility. This is especially true because of volatility. Recall that most stocks have an 'investment skew' meaning downside puts are more expensive than near the money puts in terms of volatility.

Notice, in Figure 7.3, puts get progressively more expensive in volatility terms. Let's price out a put credit versus put debit spread to see that pricing makes owning a debit spread more favorable.

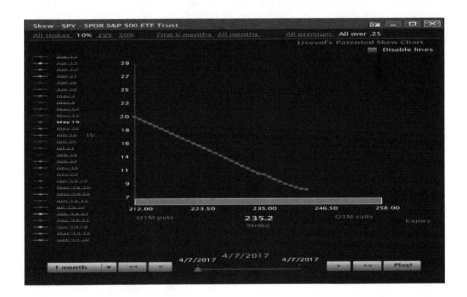

Figure 7.3: A chart of options skew in the SPY.

In this case, we are going to look at a May put spread with five weeks to expiration. In Figure 7.4, the May 2300 puts cost about 27.50, meanwhile the May 2200 puts are further out of the money and still cost more than $10. That is a huge difference in how the calls from our call discussion priced when we looked at them at a similar distance from the money. It also changes the risk-reward of a long and short put spread.

Strike	Last	PnL	Pos	SIM	Bid	Theo	Ask
SPX May19 2200	10.3				10.20	10.67	11.40
SPX May19 2205	10.2				10.70	11.20	12.00
SPX May19 2210	11.4				11.20	11.68	12.50
SPX May19 2215	10.9				11.70	12.19	13.10
SPX May19 2220	13.0				12.30	12.85	13.60
SPX May19 2225	13.4				12.90	13.35	13.90
SPX May19 2230	14.3				14.10	14.12	14.90
SPX May19 2235	14.7				14.20	14.76	15.60
SPX May19 2240	15.6				15.00	15.48	16.40
SPX May19 2245	16.7				15.80	16.29	17.30
SPX May19 2250	16.8				16.60	17.05	18.10
SPX May19 2255	17.7				17.40	17.92	18.90
SPX May19 2260	18.6				18.30	18.77	19.80
SPX May19 2265	19.0				19.20	19.66	20.80
SPX May19 2270	21.1				20.00	20.56	21.70
SPX May19 2275	22.0				21.20	21.64	22.80
SPX May19 2280	23.2				22.10	22.75	23.90
SPX May19 2285	23.8				23.30	23.91	25.00
SPX May19 2290	24.9				24.50	25.13	26.20
SPX May19 2295	26.8				25.70	26.32	27.50
SPX May19 2300	28.1				27.00	27.49	28.90

Figure 7.4: A selection of downside puts in the SPX showing option price.

I can buy or sell a put spread for about $17.50 per spread. Thus, if I buy it, I am risking $17.50 to make about $83 on the spread (Figure 7.5).

Notice that if the trader is right, this spread pays out big. However, if the trader is wrong, the $17 he or she spent goes "poof" and decays away. In owning the put debit spread the trader is looking for something to happen, just like in owning a call spread.

Looking at the put credit spread (Figure 7.6), if I sell it, I am risking $83 to make $17.

Figure 7.5: A long put spread in the SPX.

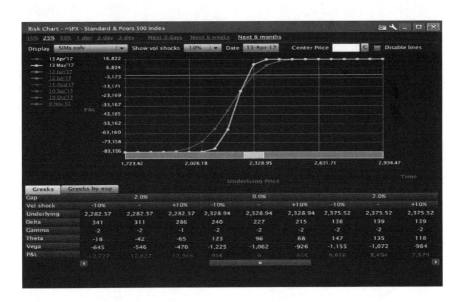

Figure 7.6: A short put spread in SPX.

The trader is betting a lot to make only a little; however, because markets tend to grind higher there are a lot of traders that like to sell put credit spreads. Traders like to bet that the market *won't* go down. The trader is looking, like a credit call spread, for something *not* to happen.

In credit versus debit spreads, it is easy to bet that nothing will happen, but the market will charge you for it if you are wrong, to the tune of over 4 to 1 most of the time. It is priced that way because generally 4 out of 10 times, nothing happens.

Credit and debit spreads are often the first spreads traders execute but they are far more complex when you sit down and think about it. Take the time to understand what makes these work and not work and you will be much better off. To wrap up credit and debit spreads:

–   A debit spread has a preference in direction of the underlying, thus it has a delta. The spread wants something to happen, thus it is long gamma. If nothing happens, the spread will lose money as time passes, thus it is short theta. The spread is buying premium; thus it wants the belief that movement will increase, making it long vega.

–   A credit spread has a preference in the direction of the underlying, thus it has a delta. The spread wants something to happen, thus it is short gamma. If nothing happens, the spread will make money as time passes, thus it is long theta. The spread is selling premium; thus it wants the belief that movement will increase, making it short vega.

The Straddle

A straddle is the buying or selling of both a call and a put on the same strike. The straddle is based on whether something will or will not happen. If you go long on a straddle, you are betting that the underlying is going to move. If you sell a straddle, you are betting that the underlying won't move.

You could describe a straddle as the perfect combo of a vega trade and a gamma trade. You want the market to think the underlying is going to start moving or stop (vega exposure) and you want the underlying to either stop or start moving (gamma exposure). Let's walk through how long and short straddles make money.

The long straddle is the purchase of a call and a put on the same strike. Looking at the P&L graph in Figure 7.7, you hope the underlying will rally. But the P&L of the position shows a 10% increase in volatility.

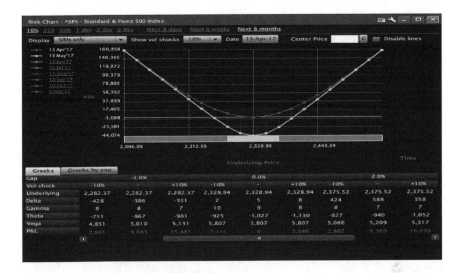

Figure 7.7: A long straddle in the SPX.

If the SPX sits, and vol goes up, you do well. If the underlying moves 2%, you do well. If the underlying moves and implied volatility increases, you hit it out of the park. If the underlying moves, even if the IV drops, you win. Gamma is a powerful force in straddles, but vega will augment the trade almost as much as the movement. In the end, you need something to happen though, either a change in perception or a change in underlying price. Wrapping up a long straddle the basic structure is:

- The spread does not have a preference in direction of the underlying, thus it is flat delta. The spread needs something to happen, thus it is long gamma. If nothing happens, the spread will lose money as time passes, thus it is short theta. The spread is buying premium; thus it wants belief that movement will increase, making it long vega.

Short Straddle

The short straddle is the opposite of the long straddle. It wants the underlying to not move and it wants perception of movement to decline. Thus, the trade is both short movement and short perception of movement. This produces a spread that is short gamma and short vega. The P&L of the short straddle in Figure 7.8 shows the preferences quite clearly.

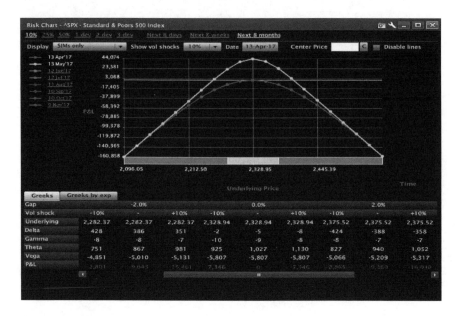

Figure 7.8: A short straddle in SPX.

The straddle loses money if the underlying moves 10%, but it loses far less if IV drops, meaning that if the underlying moves and perception of movement drops, you will be okay over time, but will lose immediately. As a straddle seller, more so than any other type of trader, you look for something *not* to happen. You want the underlying to stick either in the immediate or over time. There is an advantage for you as a straddle seller, if you have the stomach for it, if the underlying gyrates (up-and-down or down-and-up) you are in a position to do extremely well. Based on the risk associated with the straddle, I almost never sell straddles naked. Generally, I trade iron butterflies instead (I will discuss Iron Fly's later in this chapter). Wrapping up a short straddle the basic structure is:

– Short A call and a put on the same strike as in Figure 7.8
– The spread at onset does not have a preference in direction of the underlying, thus it is flat delta. The spread wants nothing to happen, thus it is short gamma. If nothing happens, the spread will make money as time passes, thus it is long theta. The spread is selling premium; thus it wants belief that movement will decrease, making it short vega.

The Strangle

A strangle, long or short, is a straddle with split strikes. The strangle takes in less premium; in return, you get a wider landing pad for the underlying to move about. Like a straddle, a strangle is vega- and gamma-centric. The strangle wants perception of movement to change and movement to change. The long strangle looks for movement and perception of movement to increase. In the example in Figure 7.9, you buy the May 2250 put and 2375 call at the same time.

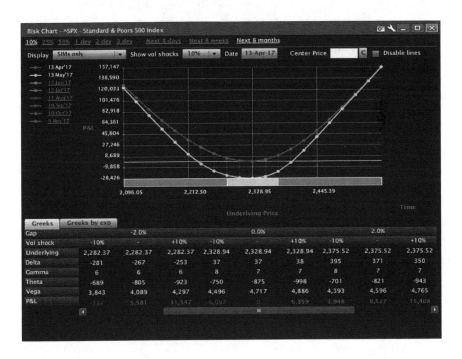

Figure 7.9: A long strangle in the SPX.

You look for movement or an increase in belief that there will be movement. You want something to happen. Wrapping up a long strangle the basic structure is:

- The spread does not have a preference in direction of the underlying, thus it is flat delta. The spread needs something to happen, thus it is long gamma. If nothing happens, the spread will lose money as time passes, thus it is short theta. The spread is buying premium; thus it wants belief that movement will increase, making it long vega.

Looking at a short straddle Figure 7.10, you are trading off a lot of risk for your belief that the underlying isn't going to move. If the underlying moves, you will lose, if the perception is that the underlying is going to move, you will lose. You are set up with a wider landing pad than a straddle, but you receive fewer dollars than a straight straddle. You receive fewer dollars (theta) relative to the straddle, but in return, the points where you lose money are much wider than a straddle.

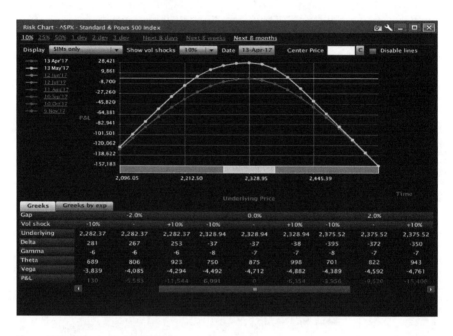

Figure 7.10: A short straddle in SPX.

You need the underlying not do something; in this case, move outside of the strikes you sold. Based on the P&L, you need the underlying to sit and the perception of movement to sit. Strangles are essentially straddles with more room whether bought or sold. Personally, I do not like buying or selling these. I think the risk-reward does not work for the independent trader. I feel similarly about straddles, but will trade them from time to time, because they are a stronger play on a hard belief. Wrapping up a short strangle, the basic structure is:

—   The spread at onset does not have a preference in direction of the underlying, thus it is flat delta. The spread wants nothing to happen, thus it is short gamma. If nothing happens the spread will make money as time passes, thus it is long theta. The spread is selling premium; thus it wants belief that movement will decrease, making it short vega.

The Iron Butterfly

An iron butterfly is simply a straddle that is hedged. You sell or buy a straddle, generally ATM (although butterflies can and often are used as directional plays). Against the straddle, you buy or sell the opposite spread in the form of a strangle. Thus, if you sell a straddle, you buy a wider strangle. If you buy the straddle, you sell the strangle against it. This lowers the premium collected or paid; in return, it lowers risks if you sell the straddle and decreases gain if you buy. I am a huge proponent of these spreads, as they can be used strategically. The added benefit of these spreads is the margin they require, which is far less than straddles, especially short straddles.

The Short Iron Butterfly

A short iron butterfly as stated above is a short strangle versus a long strangle. You look for the same result as a straddle seller, but with less cost. The longs have the effect of reducing the associated Greeks of a short straddle. Let's suppose we want to set up an iron butterfly, here is the standard way to pick strikes setting up the trade:

Start by selling an ATM straddle. Next calculate the standard deviation of the straddle. This can be done by taking the strike, multiplying it by the implied volatility of the short straddle, and then multiplying it by the square root of days to expiration of the spread, divided by the days in a calendar year. Let's look at an example starting with Figure 7.11.

Vol	Bid	Theo	Ask	SIM	Pos	PnL	Last	Strike	Last	PnL	Pos	SIM	Bid	Theo	Ask
15.25	74.4(	75.3(	77.3(				76.6!	SPX May19 2275	22.0				21.2	21.4!	22.8
15.00	70.6(	71.3(	73.1(				75.1!	SPX May19 2280	23.2				22.1	22.4!	23.9
14.79	66.8(	67.4!	69.2(					SPX May19 2285	23.8				23.3	23.6(	25.0
14.57	63.0(	63.6!	65.4(				65.2!	SPX May19 2290	24.9				24.5	24.8(	26.2
14.35	59.3(	59.9!	61.7(					SPX May19 2295	26.8				25.7	26.0!	27.5
14.14	55.7(	56.3;	58.2(				57.5(	SPX May19 2300	28.1				27.0	27.3;	28.9
13.90	52.1(	52.6!	54.4(				56.0!	SPX May19 2305	30.0				28.5	28.7;	30.2
13.67	48.6(	49.1!	50.9(					SPX May19 2310	31.2				29.9	30.2;	31.7
13.45	45.1(	45.6!	47.4(				47.2(	SPX May19 2315	33.1				31.5	31.8!	33.4
13.22	41.8(	42.4;	44.1(					SPX May19 2320	33.4				33.1	33.4(	34.9
12.96	38.6(	39.1(	40.7(				40.3!	SPX May19 2325	35.5				34.7	35.1(	36.6
12.74	35.3(	35.8(	37.5(				38.0(	SPX May19 2330	38.1				36.9	37.1(	38.4
12.45	32.3(	32.7;	34.3(				33.0(	SPX May19 2335	40.1				38.3	38.7;	40.3
12.20	29.2(	29.7!	31.4(				30.0(	SPX May19 2340	40.4				40.3	40.7!	42.3
11.96	26.5(	26.9(	28.4(				27.7!	SPX May19 2345	44.3				42.4	42.9!	44.5
11.70	23.8(	24.2;	25.6(				24.4(	SPX May19 2350	45.0				44.5	45.1(	46.8
11.41	21.0(	21.4;	22.8(				23.4(	SPX May19 2355	47.3				46.8	47.5;	49.2
11.14	18.6(	18.8!	20.0(				19.2(	SPX May19 2360	51.3				49.5	50.1(	51.7
10.91	16.2(	16.6!	17.9(				16.9(	SPX May19 2365	53.9				52.0	52.8(	54.4
10.67	14.2(	14.5!	15.7(				14.7(	SPX May19 2370	55.1				54.8	55.6(	57.2
10.40	12.1(	12.4!	13.6(				12.7(	SPX May19 2375	59.9				57.5	58.5;	60.3

Figure 7.11: Options in the SPX.

In this case, the trader would likely sell the 2325 straddle with a volatility of 12.96%; May, in this case, has 35 days to expiration. Thus, the trader would calculate the standard deviation in Excel:

2325*.1296*SQRT(35/365) or 93 points.

Obviously 93 points is a little off; 93 points will not land on a strike; thus the trader should lean in not out, making the wings 90 points wide instead of 95 points wide (wings are the long strikes on a butterfly or Iron Butterfly). Thus, the trader would set up a short iron butterfly as in the 2235–2325–2415 butterfly. However, one needs to make sure that the calls are not too cheap. If skew is steep, the calls might be inexpensive, so the trader might be buying what amounts to worthless calls as a hedge. Generally speaking, the wings should be worth at least 1–2% of the value of the underlying, generally at least 0.25 for equities and 2.50 for a major equity index. In the case above, you can see how upside calls are priced in Figure 7.12.

Vol	Bid	Thec	Ask	SIN Pos	PnL	Last	Strike
12.96	38.6(	39.0(	40.7(			40.3!	SPX May19 2325
12.74	35.3(	35.8!	37.5(			38.0(	SPX May19 2330
12.45	32.3(	32.7(	34.3(			33.0(	SPX May19 2335
12.20	29.2(	29.7!	31.4(			30.0(	SPX May19 2340
11.96	26.5(	26.9(	28.4(			27.7!	SPX May19 2345
11.70	23.8(	24.2)	25.6(			24.4(	SPX May19 2350
11.41	21.0(	21.4!	22.8(			23.4(	SPX May19 2355
11.14	18.6(	18.8!	20.0(			19.2(	SPX May19 2360
10.91	16.2(	16.6(	17.9(			16.9(	SPX May19 2365
10.67	14.2(	14.5!	15.7(			14.7(	SPX May19 2370
10.40	12.1(	12.4;	13.6(			12.7(	SPX May19 2375
10.18	10.3(	10.7(	11.8(			11.0!	SPX May19 2380
9.91	8.70	8.98	9.90			9.20	SPX May19 2385
9.70	7.20	7.56	8.50			7.78	SPX May19 2390
9.49	5.90	6.28	7.20			6.70	SPX May19 2395
9.30	4.80	5.16	6.00			5.43	SPX May19 2400
9.15	3.90	4.24	5.00			4.55	SPX May19 2405
9.01	3.10	3.46	4.20			3.65	SPX May19 2410
8.92	2.55	2.86	3.50			3.10	SPX May19 2415

Figure 7.12: Upside call pricing in the SPX.

The 2415 calls were worth about 3.00, an acceptable level for the hedged calls. Thus, the butterfly would look like Figure 7.13.

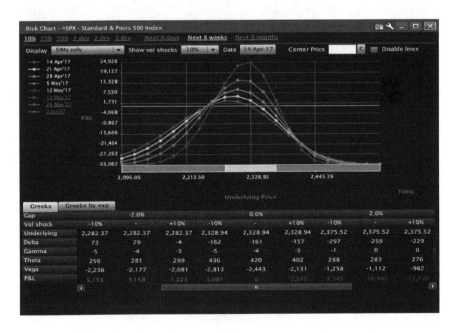

Figure 7.13: A 90 point ATM Iron Butterfly in SPX.

What you will notice is that the spread is a touch odd looking. While the strike is all set up equally, the iron butterfly appears to have a preference that the underlying should fall. This is because the delta for OTM puts is greater than that of OTM calls; this is caused by skew in the SPX options. This raises a related question that invariably affects combination strategy: Do you close profitable legs or wait to expiration? In closing one leg, the risk of the remaining side could be increased substantially. So, you need to determine (preferably in advance) whether to hold the position through to expiration in the hopes of overall profit with managed risk, or close early. In the second choice, rather than closing, rolling to a later expiration often presents the best combination of risk management and profit. At onset, we generally believe that some of the delta should be managed, so I suggest buying calls to hedge. I like buying about half of the delta, using a call inside of the 'tent' (between the short and the long) in this case, you could buy three 2375 calls to smooth out delta exposure, as shown in Figure 7.14.

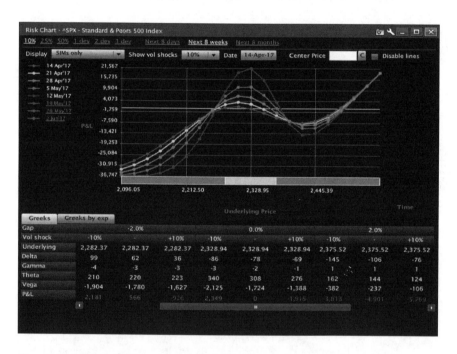

Figure 7.14: A 90 point SPX iron butterfly with delta management.

While the spread still has a delta, the gamma from the long calls reduces the true P&L effect of delta quickly because of the gamma in the calls.

With this spread on, the trader is clearly looking for one thing, the underlying to sit. If it moves, the trader will lose. Additionally, the trader is looking for the belief that the underlying might sit for a while. If the trader is right and the underlying sits as time passes, much like a short straddle, the trade is profitable. If the underlying moves, the trader will be sad. Wrapping up a short iron butterfly, the basic structure is:

— The spread does not have a preference in the direction of the underlying, thus it is flat delta once hedged. The spread wants nothing to happen, thus it is short gamma. If nothing happens the spread will make money as time passes, thus it is long theta. The spread is selling premium; thus it wants movement to decrease, making it short vega.

The Long Iron Butterfly

A long iron butterfly is developed in exactly the same way as a short iron butterfly, only on its head. The trader is buying a long straddle and using the same standard deviation formula to pick the strikes to sell. This spread has the exact opposite characteristics as well. See the example of the spread in Figure 7.15.

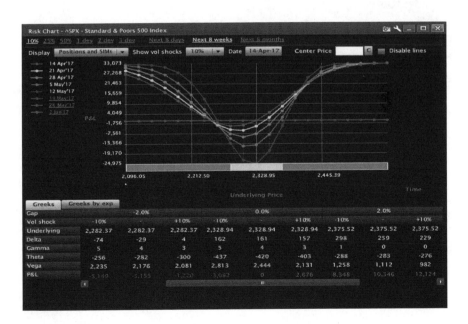

Figure 7.15: A long iron butterfly in SPX.

I do not suggest hedging off the delta of the spread, unlike in the short butterfly. This is because of the vega exposure of the spread. Because you are actually looking for movement, you need to take into account how vega will affect the value of the spread with movement. If the underlying rallies, almost certainly (except under extraordinary circumstances) IV will fall. If the underlying falls, the IV will almost certainly increase. This will change the payoff of the graph above by a wide margin, making delta the equalizer of P&L. This spread is delta neutral if you want movement to occur in either direction. You also need movement to occur quickly because the spread is purchased, thus every day that the underlying doesn't move, the trade loses money. If perception of movement increases, you will believe that the options should cost more, and the spread will make money, benefiting the trade. Wrapping up a long iron butterfly the basic structure is:

– The spread does not have a preference in direction of the underlying, thus it is flat delta. The spread needs something to happen, thus it is long gamma. If nothing happens the spread will lose money as time passes, thus it is short theta. The spread buys premium, thus it wants movement to increase, making it long vega.

Standard Butterfly

A standard butterfly is the exact same spread as an iron butterfly. The only difference is that it is made up of a long call spread and a short call spread with the shorts at the same strike, or it's a short and long put spread with the shorts at the same strike. The long call butterfly is shown in Figure 7.16; the long put butterfly is shown in Figure 7.17.

Notice that long call (Figure 7.16) and put (Figure 7.17) butterflies look almost exactly the same and share the same Greeks as the iron butterfly. This is because they are essentially the same spread.

While there are some slight differences in terms of having a call or put in the money, the spreads are synthetically (linked by put-call parity) the same spread. A long call or put butterfly ATM is going to look exactly the same as a short iron butterfly. The difference between an iron spread and the standard spread is pretty simple to calculate. Take the credit from the iron spread, subtract it from the distance between the shorts and longs and you will have the value of the call or put spread. For example, if the SPX iron butterfly that is 90 points wide and collects $57, the debit on a call or put butterfly should be 90–57 or $33 per spread.

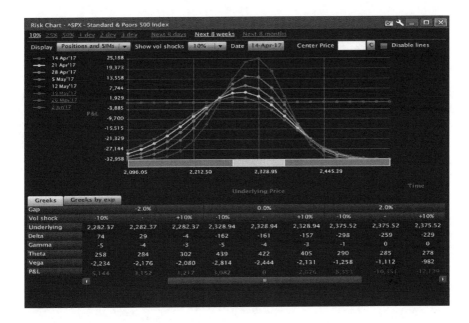

Figure 7.16: The long call butterfly.

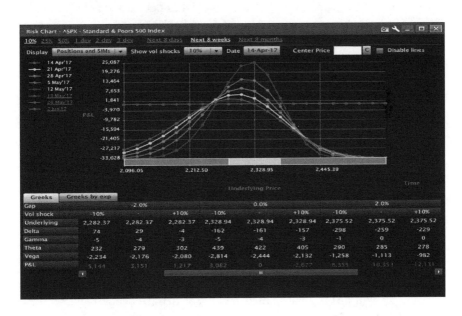

Figure 7.17: Long put butterfly in SPX.

I generally do not suggest standard ATM put butterflies, but I do like them better for directional spreads. This is primarily due to spread width of ATM versus ITM and OTM options. Here is a brief example. Take a look at the spread between the OTM calls and the ITM puts at the 2415 strike:

Vol	Bid	Thec	Ask	SIN	Pos	PnL	Last	Strike	Last	PnL	Pos	SIN	Bid	Thec	Ask
8.92	2.55	2.85	3.50				3.10	SPX May19 2415	85.4				87.1	88.7i	90.8

The OTM calls are about 0.95 wide (about 0.20–30 if quoted in the open market) while the 2415 puts are about 3.70 wide (about 0.50–70 wide if quoted in the open market). The ability to price more easily makes iron butterflies more desirable for ATM spreads in big indexes. It's worth the time to price a call and put butterfly, just in case there is a mispricing somewhere, especially in individual equities, where mispricing is more prone to happen.

The Iron Condor

An iron condor is simply a strangle that is hedged. A trader sells or buys a strangle. Against the strangle, the trader buys or sells the opposite strangle even wider than the initial strangle against the initial trade. So, if the trader sells a strangle, he or she will buy a wider strangle. If the trader buys the strangle, he or she will sell a wider strangle against it. This will lower the premium collected or paid for the strangle; in return, it will lower risk for the strangle seller and decrease the gain for the strangle buyer.

The Short Iron Condor

A short iron condor, as stated above, is a short strangle versus a long strangle. There are variants on the iron condor where one has all puts or all calls, but we almost never trade those and they are hard to find (so we are not going to discuss them). The trader is essentially looking for the same result as a strangle seller, just with less risk. The longs have the effect of reducing the associated Greeks of a short strangle. Let's suppose we want to set up an iron condor, the standard way to pick strikes consists of:

Start by figuring out what strangle to sell. For an iron condor, I typically look for wings well out of the money. I look about 60 days out and at the 10 delta mark. Next, I find options wider out that will provide the cheapest hedge in a relative sense. In 'relative sense' I mean what provides the best bang for the buck. Here are two theoretical scenarios:

I can sell the 10 delta call and put together and collect 2.50. Against it I can:
1. Buy a strangle 10 points wider for 1.50
or
2. Buy a strangle 20 points wider for 1.00

In scenario 1, I collect 1.00 (2.50–1.50), creating a margin of 900 per spread. I'm risking 900 to make 100. The payout on risks of 100/900 or 11.11% return occurs if I collect every last dollar (which I don't).

In scenario 2, I collect 1.50 (2.50–1.00), more dollars relative to scenario 1; but what about the return on risk? The payout is now 150 against the potential loss of 1850 a spread. This is a payout of 150/1850 or 8.1%.

While scenario 2 makes more raw dollars in a risk-to-reward analysis, clearly scenario 1 is preferable.

Moving on to time to expiration, in Jim Bittman's book *Trade Options Like a Professional* (2008), he discusses how selling an option 10% out of the money produces more decay in raw dollars 60 days out of the money than selling a 10% out of the money at 30 days to expiration. The way most iron condors are traded, we like setting up iron condors at about 55–70 days to expiration since that range, along with a 10 delta option sale on the condor, tends to produce optimal decay. Figure 7.18 shows a chart of an iron condor set up to these specifications:

We end up short the 2195 puts against the 2185 puts, about 7.5% OTM on the puts. The calls were sold at 2465 versus 2475, only about 4% OTM.

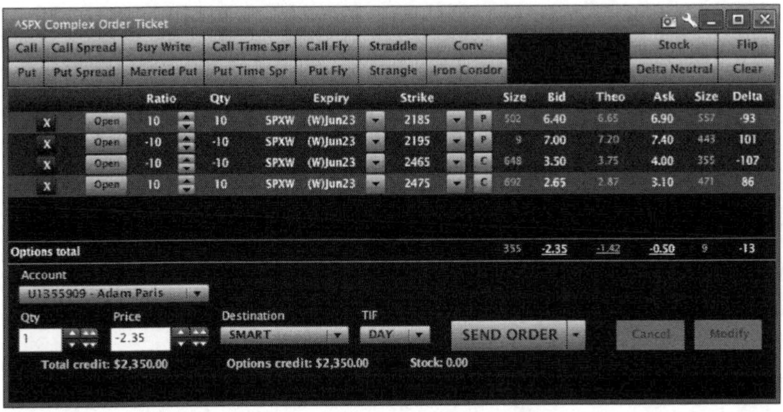

Figure 7.18: Iron Condor.

While not 10% OTM on either strike, it is at a level where, by the time the spread is 30–40 days to expiration, the decay has come out of these spreads. Interestingly, while the spread pulls more dollars out of the calls, more of the money will be made by the puts dying than the call spread. This is because of the proximity of calls relative to puts.

Risk in iron condors exists in the calls. While traders tend to obsess over downside risk in iron condors, upside risk loses more money than downside. The risk chart (Figure 7.19) makes this pretty clear:

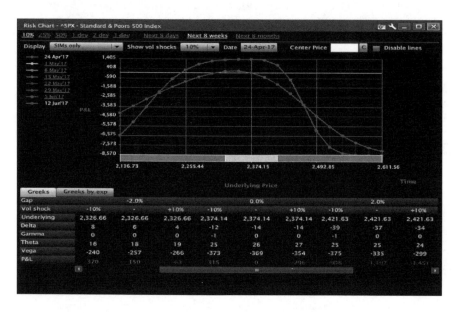

Figure 7.19: Risk chart, SPX.

Looking at risk, one can clearly see that upside options are closer and steeper. This is another reason we push traders to shoot for half the credit and to move on; the market tends to move higher creating problems in an upside condor.

We almost never trade these spreads because, as active traders, we believe we can find better values in other spreads. Those who want to trade these need to learn that these spreads are less of a sit-and-wait trade than they may seem, and are much more a play on vol dropping for a few days and collecting the vega. When we do execute these trades, we are almost never looking for more than 50% of the credit; typically, we are looking for about 30–40%, mostly derived from a drop in vol. The theta that occurs is additive. If you are in an iron condor for more than 15–20 days, you are set up to lose.

With this spread on, the trader is clearly looking for one thing, the underlying to sit. If it moves, the trader will lose. Additionally, the trader is looking for the belief that the underlying might sit for a while. If the trader is right and the underlying sits and time passes, much like a short straddle, the trade is profitable. If the underlying moves the trader will be sad (the trader loses). Wrapping up, for a short iron condor, the basic structure is:

— The spread does not have a preference in the direction of the underlying, thus it is flat delta, although it tends to have a small short delta. The spread wants nothing to happen, thus it is short gamma. If nothing happens, the spread will make money as time passes, thus it is long theta. The spread is selling premium; thus it wants movement to decrease, making it short vega.

The Calendar Spread

A calendar spread, also called a horizontal or time spread, is buying a contract in one month against selling of another contract in a different month and at the same strike (although they do not have to be). For the purposes of this description, we will assume they are on the same strike. Calendars represent a dichotomy. On one hand they want something to happen, on the other hand they do not. A long calendar spread expects the underlying to sit. The trader wants implied volatility to increase while the stock does not move at all. A short calendar spread wants just the opposite. In many ways calendars are like hedged straddles, different from the way butterflies hedge, but hedged straddles nonetheless. We will discuss how to make money on these spreads later on, but for now let's walk through the build and how they look like straddles.

The Long Calendar

A long calendar is the selling of a near-term contract and the buying of a long-term contract to set up a net debit. This can be done over weeks, months, or even over years. Traders think the long contract is cheap relative to the nearer-term short contract. When put together, the similarity to a straddle is striking, see Figure 7.20.

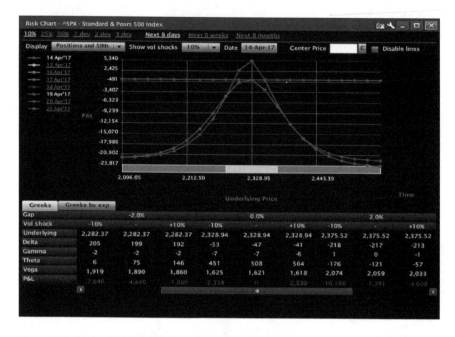

Figure 7.20: A calendar in the SPX.

The major difference is the exposure to perception in movement. The trader wants the trade to do nothing in the short term, but for long term expects movement to increase. This creates the long calendar's payouts. The longer the length between contract months the more 'perception of movement' will matter to its success.

The value of the calendar relative to the straddle beyond the 'perception of movement' exposure is the limited risk. The most a calendar spread can lose is the cost of the spread. Thus, a calendar purchased for $20 net should not lose more than the $20 paid per spread. Wrapping up a long calendar spread, the basic structure is:

— The spread does not have a preference in direction of the underlying, thus it is flat delta. The spread wants the underlying to sit, thus it is short gamma. If nothing happens, the spread will make money as time passes, thus it is long theta. The spread is buying premium; thus it wants movement to increase, making it long vega.

Short Calendar

If a long calendar is similar to a short straddle then a short calendar is going to look an awful lot like a long straddle. The short calendar is a sell of a near term option against a buy of a longer term option. It produces a spread that wants the underlying to move now, and perception of movement to fall. The trader believes that near-term options are too cheap and long-term options are too expensive. When put together, it looks a lot like a long straddle (see Figure 7.21).

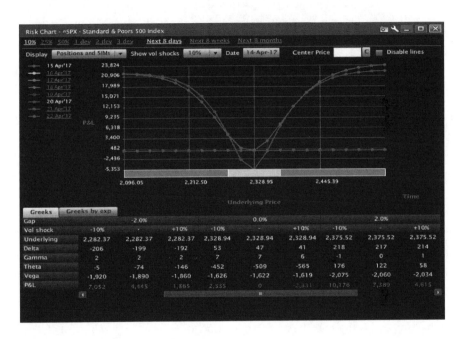

Figure 7.21: A short ATM calendar in SPX.

If the underlying moves, the trader makes money, just like a long straddle. The big difference is what the short contract represents. If perception of movement drops, the spread will make money, so it is short vega (exposure to the perception that movement will change). If the underlying moves and the perception of movement drops, the trader will do extremely well. Short calendars are great on rallies and less than great on sell-offs. I like the spreads; however, the downside of the short calendar is that despite the limited risk, they are generally margined worse than long straddles. Many firms view the short strike as naked despite the fact that it's hedged by near term options.

The one issue with these spreads is if the trader is wrong on perception of movement. If the back month begins to see an increase in movement perception, the P&L of the short calendar can change quickly, creating problems for the trader. A big increase in the long-term option can cause losses to be greater than the initial P&L predicts, and can be so large that the longer-term option can possibly see its value increase.

Wrapping up a short calendar spread the structure is:
- The spread does not have a preference in direction of the underlying, thus it is flat delta. The spread wants the underlying to move, thus it is long gamma. If nothing happens the spread will lose money as time passes, thus it is short theta. The spread is selling premium; thus it wants belief that movement will decrease, making it short vega.

Front and Back Spreads

Front and back spreads involve the trading of one option near the money against the trading of several options out of the money. Depending on the spreads, they want either a long movement (back spread) or almost no movement (front spread). These are considered professional trades as they tend to be margin intensive. We will dig into these in detail in later chapters, but I want to spend a few moments describing these trades.

Back Spreads

A back spread is the sale of a near-term option to finance the purchase of at least two options out of the money. The spread uses the near-the-money option to finance the further-out-of-the-money options in hopes of rapid movement from the underlying. These spreads generally do have a directional bias, but can be set up not to lose if the underlying moves in the opposite direction, so long as they are set up for a credit or for zero cost. These spreads, more than any other spread, require a change in perception *with* a change in movement. If the underlying moves in the direction of the spread, the trader will likely not make money, but if the underlying moves and perceptions change, the trade will do exceptionally well. These are usually set for periods when IV is perceived to be cheap. A classic example would be for the spread to be executed for even money. Let's look at an example in SPX, in this case short 10 SPX 2350s versus long 20 SPX 2380 calls, as shown in Figure 7.22.

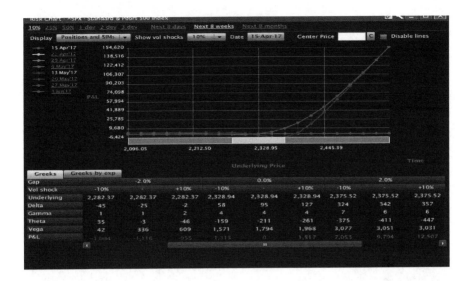

Figure 7.22: A long back spread in SPX.

Notice that as time passes, the spread loses exposure to movement and the spread becomes less effective. Back spreads need movement and they prefer it quickly, preferably with an increase in perception of movement. They can be set up as either bullish or bearish. To do them at zero cost in equities and indexes, generally call back spreads will have strikes closer than put back spreads (caused by skew). Wrapping up a long back spread, the basic structure is:

- The spread does not have a preference in direction of the underlying, thus it is flat delta; but in the end, expects the underlying to move in the direction of the long strike. The spread needs something to happen, thus it is long gamma. If nothing happens, the spread will lose money as time passes, thus it is short theta. The spread is buying premium; thus it wants belief that movement will increase, making it long vega.

The Front Spread

A front spread is a flip of the back spread, and often is called the 'pro' trade because it is so popular among professional traders. The trader buys a near-the-money option and sells at least two out-of-the-money options. The spread is almost always set up as a credit. The goal of the trade is for the underlying to slowly creep toward the two short strikes, but not get there quickly. As time passes, the OTM options lose Greeks and the near-the-money options gain delta and gamma. What is odd about a front spread is that the trader wants movement, just extremely slow movement. If the underlying moves slowly toward the short strike, the trade will do extremely well. If the underlying moves too hard, the trade loses. Generally, these are done as a credit, so if they move in the opposite direction of the spread, they will make money for the trader. Essentially, the value of a front spread is that the trader can be right or wrong and still win, as long they aren't *too* right. A call front spread is shown in Figure 7.23.

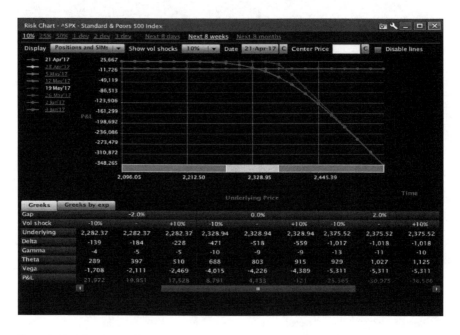

Figure 7.23: A front spread in SPX.

With the underlying trading 2325, the trader is long 10 of the 2350 calls and short 20 of the 2375s for a net credit. If the underlying creeps higher, the trader does well. If the underlying drops, the trader keeps the credit. The issue the trader will have is if the underlying rallies quickly, above 2375, the P&L starts to look ugly. Bear spreads tend to be wider because of skew, and bullish spreads will have to be tighter if done for a credit. Wrapping up a front spread, the basic structure is:

- The spread at onset does not have a preference in direction of the underlying, thus it is flat delta; but in the end, wants the underlying to slowly move in the direction of the short strikes. The spread needs movement to be slow, thus it is short gamma. If nothing happens, the spread will make money as time passes, thus it is long theta. The spread is selling premium; thus it wants belief that movement will drop, making it short vega.

Chapter 8
Adding Edge to Spreads

The last chapter reviewed many option spreads. In this chapter, the discussion centers on how spreads can have edge to them, *not* the structure of the trade. Many books present the latter, but few give you the former. In this chapter, the basic spread is presented as a trade with edge.

Credit/Debit Spreads

A *credit* vertical spread involves a purchase of one option and a sale of another with the same expiration, but different strike prices, where the sold option is closer to the money than the bought option. This produces a net credit. A debit spread, on the other hand, is a spread combining a long option closer to the money, with a short option, setting up a net debit.

The assumed set of positions in this description is to set up a spread out of the money. In other words, with calls, the positions would be close to the money combined with a higher strike, and with puts, the spread would combine close-to-the-money positions with lower strikes. As an issue of risk, the 'moneyness' of the strikes are crucial and risk is well managed with OTM short positions. However, by definition, a vertical spread could also include deep ITM options, adding to exercise risk in exchange for higher short premium receipts (meaning a lower debit or a higher credit). The offset to these desirable adjustments in premium levels is inevitably not justified by higher risks. And so, in the discussion that follows, the assumption is that we're talking about close-to-the-money spreads.

To begin on the comparison, the spreads represented in Figures 8.1 and 8.2 are essentially the same. Why? Because rather than making a distinction between credit and debit spreads, it is more realistic to define vertical positions as either call spreads or put spreads.

When placed next to each other, these two spreads are the same in terms of risk. Professional traders do not look at these spreads as credit and debit spreads; instead they typically view each of the spreads as a call spread or a put spread. A *call spread* is a trade that is set up above the strike at the money. You may sell a call credit spread, or buy a call debit spread out of the money; in either case, you have opened a call spread. You may buy a *put spread* out of the money (a long below the ATM price), creating a long put spread, or execute the opposite to set up a short put spread.

https://doi.org/10.1515/9781501505676-008

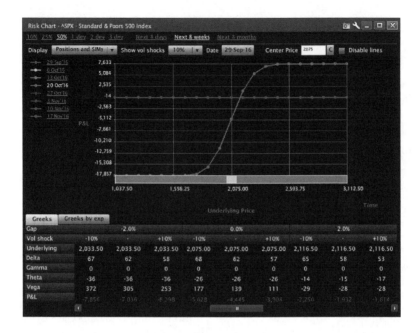

Figure 8.1: SPX, trading 2150, 2125-2100 Credit Spread.

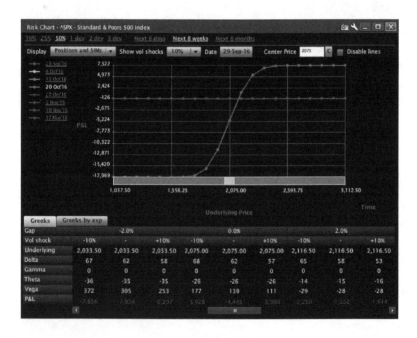

Figure 8.2: SPX trading 2150, 2125-2100 Debit Spread.

The difference between a short spread and a long spread is the opinion you are expressing about likely direction. If you put on a spread, you need to decide if the underlying is going to move in the desired direction (toward the long strike), or *not* move in that direction, away from the strike. If you sell a spread, you expect that movement to *not* happen.

Figure 8.2 is the chart for a sale of an SPX 2125 put versus a buy of a 2100 put (a short put spread). With the S&P 500 trading 2150, if you sell the 2125-2100 put spread at 7.65, you assume that the SPX will not fall below 2125 and, at a minimum, not fall below 2125-7.65 or 2117.35. The easy way to think about selling a put or call spread is that you want the underlying *not* to move in the direction of the spread. When you are rooting against movement, you assume that volatility will drop. Thus, a sale of a call or put spread assumes the underlying will *not move*.

If both options are in the money—meaning the moneyness is moved higher in a call spread or lower in a put spread—you increase the risk on the short side, so this must rely on rapid *time decay* (the ratio of the change in an option's price to the decrease in time to expiration). For this reason, the time remaining to expiration should be very fast, 10 days or less, for example. However, this makes it more difficult for the long side to become profitable, because of the same time decay issues. This problem illustrates why the most likely positions to generate profits should center around the current price, with one side slightly above and the other slightly below. This simply is the most realistic scenario to generate profits.

This is a mindset you may adopt with risk awareness at the core of how you pick strikes. Position and proximity define whether you expect movement to happen (thus setting up long vol), or not to happen (thus setting up short vol). With this thinking, if you are *long*, you want the underlying to move in that direction for a call spread or put spread. A long call equals upward bias, and a long put equals downward bias.

Look at the opposite of my put spread from above. If I could sell the spread at 7.65, that means I could buy the spread close to that price as well (with adjustments between bid and ask prices). Whereas the short put spread expected the underlying to stay above 2117.35, in this case the expectation is for the underlying to drop. Thus, you anticipate a move lower to 2117.35 by expiration.

Figure 8.3 shows a purchase of the 2125 put versus a sale of the 2100 put. You expect the underlying to move, since you need movement, as you are long volatility.

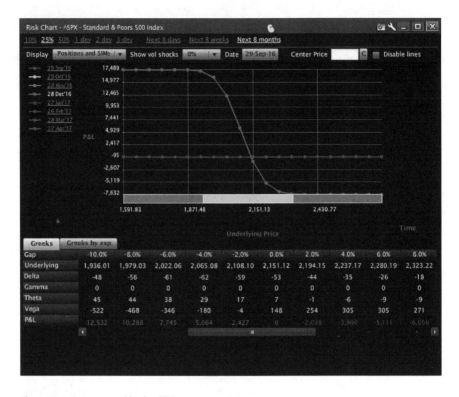

Figure 8.3: A put spread in the SPX.

How do you create a call or put spread with edge? The answers:
1. Volatility
2. Skew
3. Management

Volatility

When going long or short, the first thing you need is to determine in what direction volatility is going. If IV is super low or on the rally, or price is on the rally, think about taking advantage of the change in movement or the change in volatility. This is done by buying a spread as opposed to selling it. The anticipation is that the increase in vol or movement will result in a quick profit (this is shown for AAPL in Figure 8.4).

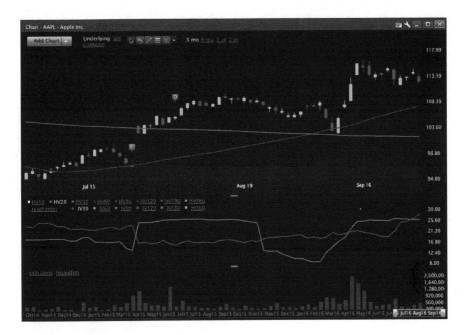

Figure 8.4: AAPL Stock price (top) IV and 20-day historical volatility.

In this example, both price and IV were increasing. If you think the underlying is going to go up, set up a long call or call spread, and if you think the underlying is going to drop, do the opposite. Next, look at Figure 8.5, the chart of TAP (Molson-Coors):

Figure 8.5 shows that IV has plummeted and HV (movement over the last 20 days of trading), while having rallied, started to flatten and dip lower. This might be a setup for a short spread. If movement dies, whether you are playing the underlying drop or rally, consider a sale, as it appears the above movement (as seen in a rise in HV20) is going to drop.

In playing volatility, you set up a trade you believe more likely to succeed in confirming your opinion on the stock's direction. Avoid the trap of selling spreads when the underlying is moving, or buying spreads in a stock not moving. If you convert the opinion into a will-move or won't-move decision, you create edge in the trade.

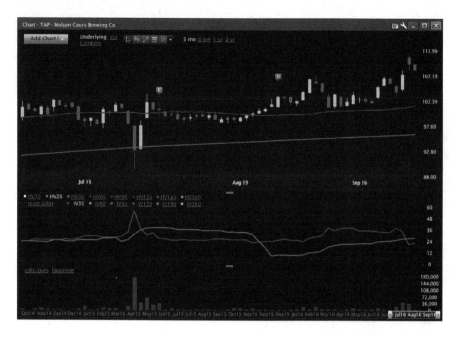

Figure 8.5: Molson-Coors stock price, IV and HV showing divergence.

Skew

The next part of evaluating volatility is an examination of skew. Skew describes how calls and puts are related, and represents the curve of the entire product when it gets out of whack due to sudden changes in volatility. Look at the TAP curve in Figure 8.6, where the Y axis is IV and the X axis is strike price.

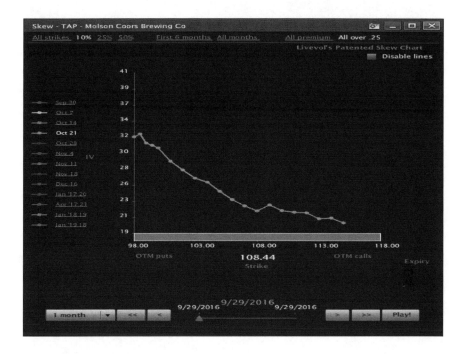

Figure 8.6: The skew curve of TAP.

There is a slight kink in the TAP curvature at 104. The 104 strike puts are too expensive relative to the 105 and the 103 strikes. If you are inclined to sell a put spread, the 104's are the strike to sell in October. Against a sale of the 104 puts, you can buy any contract below 103. In this case, if you sell the 104 strike (which is too expensive) you are buying cheap, relatively. As long as you sell the 104 puts, any purchase will create 'edge in the trade.' This is because you capture the overpriced vol from the 104s by buying against them. Now look at the option montage in Figure 8.7.

Strike	Last	PnL	Pos	SIM	Bid	The	Ask	Vo	IV	Del
TAP Oct21 97.5	0.40				0.30	0.37	0.45	33.	33.	8.8
TAP Oct21 98	0.35				0.30	0.37	0.45	32.	32.	9.1
TAP Oct21 98.5					0.35	0.45	0.55	32.	32.	10.
TAP Oct21 99	0.40				0.40	0.45	0.50	31.	31.	10.
TAP Oct21 99.5					0.40	0.50	0.60	31.	31.	11.
TAP Oct21 100	0.60				0.45	0.55	0.65	30.	30.	13.
TAP Oct21 101					0.50	0.60	0.70	28.	28.	14.
TAP Oct21 102					0.60	0.70	0.80	27.	27.	17.
TAP Oct21 103					0.70	0.82	0.95	26.	26.	20.
TAP Oct21 104	0.95				0.95	1.02	1.10	26.	26.	24.
TAP Oct21 105	1.10				1.10	1.20	1.30	24.	24.	28.
TAP Oct21 106	1.25				1.30	1.42	1.55	23.	23.	33.
TAP Oct21 107	1.50				1.60	1.72	1.85	22.	22.	39.
TAP Oct21 108	1.85				2.00	2.10	2.20	22.	22.	45.
TAP Oct21 109	2.60				2.40	2.52	2.65	21.	21.	52.

Figure 8.7: A montage of October puts in TAP.

The Oct 104-100 put spread collects about 0.47 of the cash per spread. The 105-100 spread collects about 0.65, that is 0.18 more, and the 103-100 spread collects 0.27, or 0.20 less than the 104-100. The difference between the three strikes is 0.19 per strike—(0.20 + 0.18)/2—if the curve was smooth, but in this case 0.02 has moved to the 104 strike. Thus, that is the strike to sell.

In the above example, if vol were reversed and you thought the underlying was going to move, you would want to do the opposite. With the underlying around 108, you should buy the 108 to the 105 strike and sell the 104 strike to create maximum curvature with real premium; you want to sell the 104s against any long put purchase because the 104s are too expensive.

Alternatively, look at the curve of TAP options in Figure 8.8.

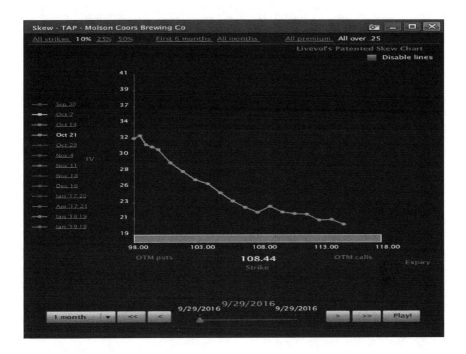

Figure 8.8: The October skew curve of TAP.

You could buy any strike other than the 104s (because they are too expensive) and sell a strike below 100. Avoid buying strikes that are bid and avoid selling strikes that are offered, which means avoid buying options out of whack with a high vol and avoid selling options out of whack below the curve. Utilizing the skew curve is crucial in picking strikes almost all the time. In some other spreads, other factors are involved relative to credit and debit spreads; the best way to create edge is with skew, followed by volatility.

Management

With call and put spreads, the key to management is to get paid the right amount for the trade and then get out. Understanding how the Greeks change as time passes becomes key. Early on in the trade with a credit and debit spread, assuming it's not executed the week of expiration, the two strikes are similar. As time passes, long and short strikes act less alike. This is seen in how the payout moves with time in the near-the-money call spread shown in Figure 8.9. Notice how the P&L curve becomes steeper as time passes.

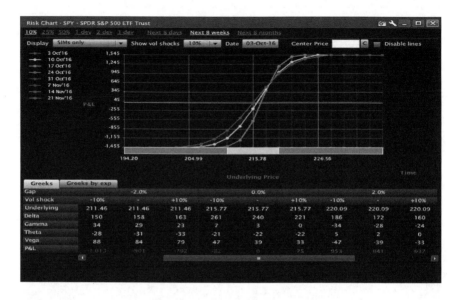

Figure 8.9: Note how the payout moves in a near-the-money call spread.

As the curve becomes steeper, what is really happening is that is the near-the-money option retains gamma and delta, while the out-of-the-money option is losing those Greeks. The effect and lesson of this is that the underlying needs to rally further away from the short strike in order for the spread to reach max profit. Early on, however, it will become profitable on smaller movement

When managing a call or put spread, take into account what the P&L curve looks like at the outset, and what your profit targets are (or should be) based on this curve. The number one mistake is being too greedy or setting unrealistic expectations. For long call and put spreads, here is the risk management approach we use at Option Pit:

1. Don't look for more than 100% return on margin.
2. Gun for 50-75% of margin.
3. If the spread makes half the profit target in the first day or two, close the trade.
   a. The trade likely was done for a greater edge than you realized and has come out of the trade; take the money and run.
4. Set a loss target at *less* than the profit target.
   a. Win 50% of the time and make more than you lose, and you will be profitable.
5. Never lose more than what you expect to make.

6. If you make an adjustment on the spread, the original margin is still where maximum loss should be set.
7. It is okay to add to a trade, not to average down.
    a. Adding to a trade is *liking* the trade more at a better price. Market makers do this all the time.
    b. Averaging down is saying, "I liked it for a dollar, I must *love* it for 0.50," whether the trade is still good or not.
8. If the conditions or the assumptions change, *get out!*

A Few Words on Adjusting

You adjust spreads by buying in the opposite direction as expected underlying movement. Buying options in the opposite direction allows you to buy premium in a name that you *thought* premium should be bought. Someone bought a call or put spread because they thought premium was cheap *and* had a directional bias.

You will want to sell spreads or options if volatility pops. If this pop occurs before you sell, make sure that assumptions did not change. If you sell, you need to have a strong opinion on direction, because if vol pops and the direction is wrong, selling turns a bad trade into a stink bomb. We do *not* sell spreads against long spreads at Option Pit.

The following list shows what we do at Option Pit for short call and put spreads:
1. Set profit target at 50% of the credit or less.
2. If the spread makes half the profit target in the first day or two, get out.
3. Set loss at the profit target.
4. If you adjust the spread, the original margin is still where the maximum loss should be set.
5. Add to the trade, but do so at different strikes; *never* average down.
6. If conditions change or the assumptions change, get out.

Generally speaking, when you sell spreads as the underlying moves against you, you will slowly buy to close the short option in order to control delta. This ensures that the net trade still has a credit.

In adjusting, we push to cut delta by one-third to one-half, typically adjusting to the delta of the original trade.

If you cannot cut delta by the desired level and maintain a credit, the trade was the wrong trade and we made a mistake on the spread.

We will see this approach to management and adjusting for other spreads over and over again. We are believers in hammering the point.

Chapter 9
Butterflies and Condors

Beyond basic call and put spreads, the interesting next step is trading butterflies and condors. Much of what goes into a call or put spread creates a good butterfly or iron condor. And just as with a call or put spread, creating a butterfly or condor with edge demands a firm grasp of three matters:
1. Volatility
2. Skew
3. Management

In piecing these together, you create a butterfly or condor with high odds of success, even with an ATM spread, because you will trade with edge. The key is to use the information in front of you to piece the right trade together, both in choosing the right spread and in identifying strikes and expiration for maximum potential.

The Butterfly

The basic butterfly is illustrated in Figure 9.1. In concept, a butterfly utilizes the following conditions:
1. Short implied volatility
2. Short realized volatility
3. Centering around one strike

What other trade performs that way? A butterfly is simply a straddle that is hedged if the underlying moves. Straddles are executed by maximizing volatility or lack of volatility. Here is a graph of a short straddle.

https://doi.org/10.1515/9781501505676-009

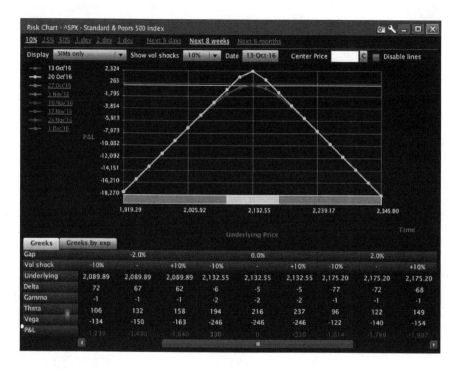

Figure 9.1: A short straddle.

If the underlying moves hard, your losses are largely stomped out because of the hedge. An *iron butterfly* (a straddle sold ATM with a wider strangle set up as a hedge) looks like the comparison in Figure 9.2; this one is set with wings 50 points wide.

The Greeks of the two trades are revealing. Both trades begin with:
- short gamma
- long theta
- short vega

The butterfly has the least extreme Greeks. The trade is about half as sensitive to movement, time, and volatility as a straddle. Interestingly, it does not give up nearly as much upside as half of the short straddle. So, what makes these trades winners? For a straddle, the answer is easy: if the underlying sits or only moves around a bit, you win. A butterfly is not nearly as easy, since you can use the other pieces of the trade to create spreads with a greater chance of success than that of a straddle. What makes a good butterfly?

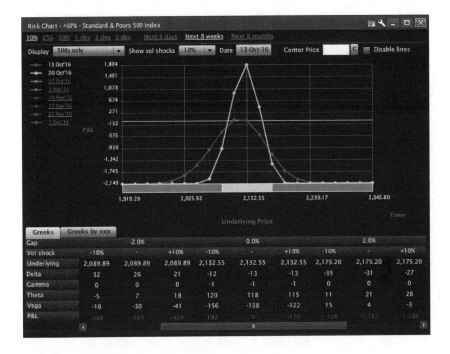

Figure 9.2: An iron butterfly with wide wings.

Trading a Butterfly

To start a trade in a butterfly, it should first have falling IV. The butterfly is short vega; this means the trade has volatility exposure. If IV falls, the butterfly will make money quickly as its vega exposure delivers. In Figure 9.3 a butterfly sees a 10% drop in IV ATM in one day.

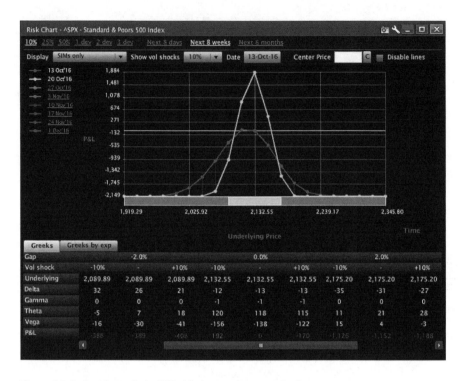

Figure 9.3: A short butterfly in SPX with day 1 and near expiration payouts.

With a drop in volatility of 10%, the butterfly made $192 on risk of $2,149, net of commissions (you can see the 10% drop category under 0% move; P&L moves from zero to $192 on a drop, almost 10% on the trade with just a move in vol). Given a day or two of decay after this event, the trade is likely to close. When we discuss risk management, we argue that with a 10% drop in vol and *no* time passing, the above trade is a close. If IV falls immediately, thus trending down, that is favorable to a butterfly.

The next key is movement. What is going on with the underlying? Is it decreasing or increasing? It's okay to execute a butterfly if IV is up, but if movement is also up, it's a terrible idea. If movement is stable or falling, investigate further. Why is implied volatility increasing? If a butterfly is a bad idea, it's because IV is rising or movement is rising, a real problem for these spreads. If movement is falling and IV is falling as seen as in Figure 9.3, it makes sense to trade a butterfly, otherwise you would need to believe that price levels were going to fall. Figure 9.4 is a chart showing a price (top) IV movement and HV movement in the S&P 500 (SPX). It might have been a perfect butterfly candidate. Over the 6 months shown in Figure 9.4, the underlying was unable to keep up with IV. If IV is going to hang out above movement that long, a butterfly might be appropriate.

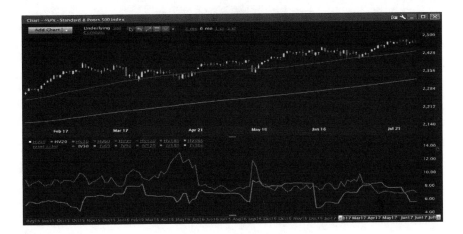

Figure 9.4: SPX price (top) IV and HV over a six month period.

That being said, I would not be 'all over' butterfly trading in SPX in this case. The reason is that IV was rising starting in June and rallying quickly. Very rarely does IV make a big move higher and then stop. We know that IV tends to correlate to itself. In other words, when IV rallies it tends to keep rallying and when IV drops it tends to keep dropping. Knowing this, what does a butterfly expect to happen? It expects IV to drop. If you execute a butterfly, be aware that if IV is rallying it probably won't work. In addition, IV is meant to be a leading indicator of movement. Even though it is not particularly accurate, and almost always overpriced, this doesn't mean you should unload butterflies into rising IV, because IV close to 50% of the time leads to a nice pop in volatility.

If you trade butterflies, be on top of volatility and how it is acting at the time; it should be falling, not rallying, hopefully from a level not overly sold (low). See the chart in Figure 9.5 for Citigroup.

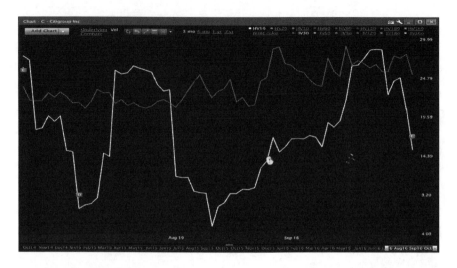

Figure 9.5: Citigroup IV and 10 day HV.

If IV falls with movement, that may be the best time to execute a butterfly. However, there is one other factor important to the success of a trade: skew. A skew chart is shown in Figure 9.6.

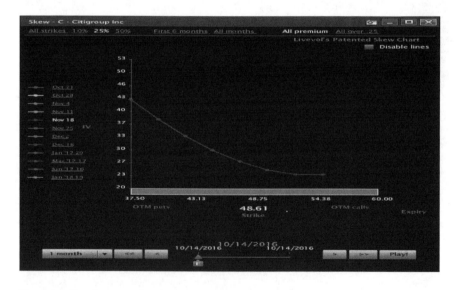

Figure 9.6: The skew curve in C.

The speed of IV increase on puts relative to calls is clear. Puts, options below the strike, tend to be sensitive to IV movement, but can also move on their own. When running tests on butterflies, how overpriced is the downside of the curve? If puts are expensive, the iron butterfly is going to be cheap (the standard butterfly will be too expensive). We trade straddles because the IV is expensive. We trade butterflies because the IV is too expensive, and because it is cheap to buy the downside. If puts are cheap, the butterfly is cheap and the trade will probably make money. To trade butterflies effectively, you cannot pay too much for downside puts. Cheap puts produce an iron butterfly that collects more profit and a standard butterfly that is too cheap.

Sounds easy, right? The problem is that it can be difficult to spot cheap vol and skew. The key is to be on top of volatility and curvature (skew). If curvature is cheap, even if IV is low, the trade may still be good; the opposite tends not to be true. The moral of the story is that skew (curvature) makes butterflies succeed.

The final step is picking strikes in an environment where HV and IV are falling and skew is normal or flat. Review the curve and find the best strikes to buy and sell. Look at the curve in VIX in Figure 9.7.

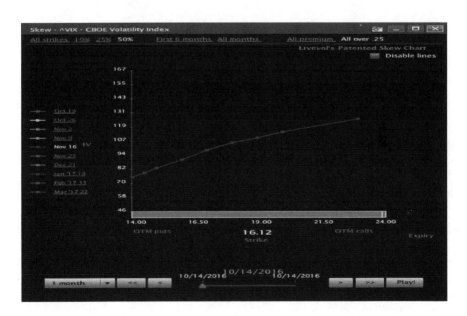

Figure 9.7: The skew curve in VIX.

Some strikes are expensive and some are cheap. In the case of VIX, you would need to buy the 19s and 17s and sell the 18s. That would create a better butterfly from a price perspective. Compare, knowing the underlying is about $17.35. Comparing the 18–19–20 butterfly to the 17–18–19 butterfly, the value difference is apparent.

Consider the 18–19–20 iron butterfly discussed in the previous paragraph. It creates a credit of about 0.90. The17–18–19 discussed above creates a credit of 0.95. When the trade is this close to the money and this tight, there is little difference between the two trades, yet one produces a better price by0.05, which is a lot of edge for a trade of this width. You apply vol and skew concepts to pick strikes with an extra 0.05 on a tight spread, meaning you will have a hard time losing money on the trade.

The checklist for butterflies:
1. Sinking movement
2. Sinking IV
3. Flat skew
4. Picking the right strikes

Targeting Profit in a Butterfly

Once you put the butterfly on, the goal is the to make a quick dollar. Look for 10–15% on margin; if you want to get aggressive, shoot for 20%. On the other end, if managing losses, never accept a loss greater than what you are gunning for in wins. Win the same amount as you lose and win more often. The alternative is to win more than you lose and then make the same as you might lose. Either works, but you want to win, not lose.

Condors

Much of what makes a butterfly a successful trade makes a condor successful as well. While a butterfly is very similar to a short straddle, a condor is much more like a short strangle. Compare the two spreads in Figures 9.8 and 9.9.

Strangle

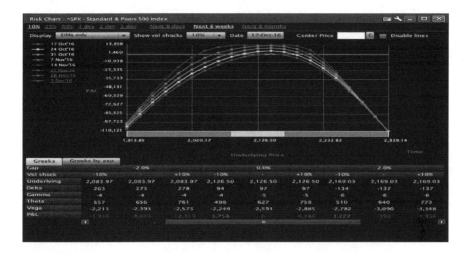

Figure 9.8: Strangle.

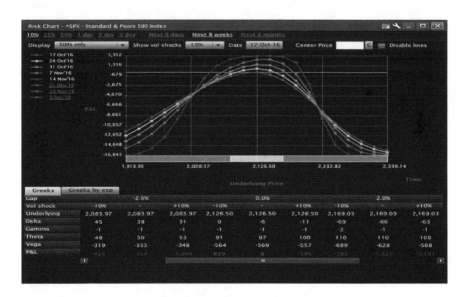

Figure 9.9: A risk graph of a condor in SPX.

At expiration, because of the long wings (long options against the short options), there is a difference in how much money can be lost in a disaster; at their onset and within the short strike, the two spreads have similar characteristics. Much like a butterfly's P&L, the success of the trade is decided by whether HV is sinking, whether IV is sinking, and whether you can get the best price on the spread as a whole. However, the roles of IV, HV, and skew for a condor are slightly different than for the butterfly.

IV and HV

Like a butterfly, the condor expects HV and IV to fall; it will perform best under those circumstances. The difference in execution between the condor and the butterfly has to do with range. While a butterfly expects the underlying to stop completely, a condor is much more forgiving of movement. The distance between the short strikes leaves room for the underlying to move around. This makes the spread great for choppy markets, where you can capture IV spikes *and* have room for the underlying to move on a reaction and IV to drop.

Retail condor traders often believe that because IV is overpriced naturally, that makes condors a perfect spread to trade. The problem is that low HV might also be in conjunction with momentum. With a condor, you look for a choppy market that might have a slightly higher movement, but the underlying is spinning wheels (going nowhere).

A market where wheels spin is perfect for a condor because there will be opportunities to execute the sale on a lower spin and carry the trade as it rallies. Within one spin, the trader may be able to get out of the iron condor trade.

Several periods are perfect for condors that might not look as perfect on the basis of HV alone. To see this effect, overlay an indicator such as Bollinger Bands to visualize HV. The chart in Figure 9.10 demonstrates this point, specifically for periods where HV is declining. If you sold a condor in mid-August it might have gotten stuck or whipsawed by the market. If you were to sell in mid-September in the middle of a huge candle caused, say, by fear Deutsche Bank was going to go bust, but you believed that Deutsche Bank was going to be all right, you could have executed a condor and been in a position to collect a lot of chop and be out of a condor for a profit.

Figure 9.10: A price chart of SPX.

Meanwhile, look at the HV in Figure 9.11.

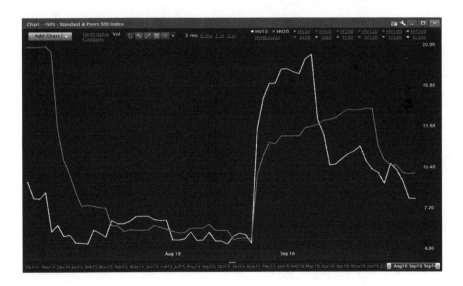

Figure 9.11: 10 and 20 day HV in SPX around the Deutsche Bank scare.

IV is cut and dried: if it's dropping, it's good for a condor, as well as for a butterfly. The big difference is that a condor can take a little more change in IV relative to a butterfly. Where a butterfly seeks a thumping of implied volatility, a condor is better with a 'melt,' meaning the underlying is doing little to nothing or chopping in a range, and is a trade that makes sense when there is a chance that IV still has more chop to it. Like a butterfly, condor trades expect a sinking of option premiums.

Skew

The big difference between a condor and a butterfly is the use of skew in analyzing the trade. While a butterfly necessarily makes money because of the skew, a condor relies less on curvature to succeed. That does not mean that you should ignore the skew curve. Skew is especially useful in condors for strike selection, which is visualized in the curve and makes a big difference by helping you decide what options to buy and sell. While a few pennies here and there can make little difference on an individual basis, making a few extra dollars on every trade over time creates a system of consistent profits.

Look at the curve in Figure 9.12.

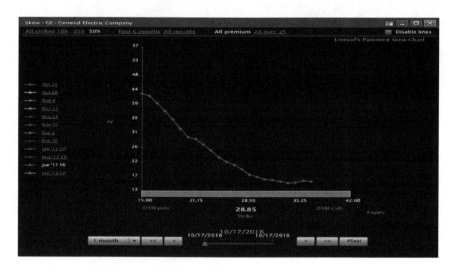

Figure 9.12: The Skew curve for January options in GE.

In this curve of GE options, there is a kink in the downside curve. You can sell the 22.50s and buy the 20 puts at nearly the same volatility. This is the type of trade that makes a condor profitable over time. By selling the same volatility on the put portion of the curve, you collect more premium. In an equity index, the lower the strike, the higher the IV. If you buy and sell the same IV, you collect more premium than you would expect otherwise. More premium means a greater credit, which in turn means higher odds of success.

Set Up and Management

Like the butterfly, there are many ways to set up a condor depending on style. In managing a condor, follow the same rules as a butterfly. Never try to make too much, never lose more than you are trying to make. In adjusting, make trades that reduce risk, not ones that strap on risk.

Follow these guidelines for setting up a condor:
1. Look for falling HV and a choppy market
2. Look for falling IV
3. Take advantage of skew to set up the trade
4. Manage the position
5. Exit the trade

In the end, much like a butterfly, if you follow the steps to put on a good trade, you will win more often than not, and you will have an easier time managing risk.

Chapter 10
The Front Spread

The *front spread* shares many characteristics with butterflies and bull call spreads, except that they are set up as naked trades or with off-center strikes. Here at Option Pit, we love these trades for several reasons:

1. They enable put or call selling at extremes without being completely naked
2. They have a directional bias but are not extremely directional
3. They collect premium
4. They are short volatility
5. They improve with time

There are a few things that make front spreads different from and, in my opinion, superior to butterflies and short call and put spreads. More often than not, when I look at trades at Option Pit, I end up with a broken wing butterfly or front spread. The trade is going to do well based on specific volatility conditions and, to a lesser extent, on skew conditions. The trade also tends to rely on moderate directional bias.

What Is a Front Spread?

When I was a floor trader, I preferred trading any option that was short gamma and long theta (a trade that expected little or no movement and collected on time decay). To the institutional and retail public, a front spread is a very specific trade that we call a 1 by 2. This means you are long '1' option (purchased for a debit). At the same time, you set up a credit in the '2' part of the 1 by 2. For example, you're long one option that is close to the money for 2 dollars; and you are short 2 options further away from the money, at 1.25. The net is 2 long less (2 x 1.25) 2.50 short, for a net credit on the 1 by 2 of 0.50. − $2 − ($1.25 x 2) = 0.50 credit. The *2 refers to the short positions.

This trade gains exposure in the direction you expect the underlying to move, and you get paid to set up the trade. However, you are at risk in this trade if the underlying moves too hard or too fast. If your trade moves beyond the *range* you set, your position could lose big. The risk graph is shown in Figure 10.1.

https://doi.org/10.1515/9781501505676-010

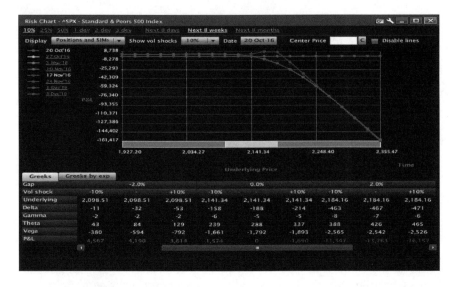

Figure 10.1: The P&L payout of the purchase of one ATM call and the sale of two further OTM calls.

The position expects the underlying to move higher. If expiration is above 2140, the position makes more than it would if the underlying is lower. It doesn't expect movement to be too quick. As more time passes, the more you hope the underlying will move higher. A move early is a loser but, with time, a run higher does well. At no point in time do you want a strong move in the direction of the trade. Why? At the onset, the trade's delta is opposite of what you want as time passes; the trade is short delta and expecting the underlying to drop. As time passes, you expect the underlying to rally and delta to become positive. This is caused by the two short options losing value from theta and becoming closer to worthless near expiration. This is an effective trade if managed properly.

Creating a Front Spread

The key to an effective front spread is forming an opinion on direction. The beauty of this trade is that it can be set up against the direction or with the direction. It is the classic 'fade' set up or the classic 'slow down' trade. Decide the trade by relying on one thing: volatility.

Let's look at an example of both.

IV

The USO chart shown in Figure 10.2 had IV points and exploded, but the underlying was finding a floor.

Figure 10.2: Stock price and IV of the USO ETF.

The lower graph saw a peak at the same time the top graph was in the trough. IV exploded as the underlying dropped (between July and August). At those points, when IV was at its peak and the underlying was dropping, a bear 1 by 2 put spread would allow you to take advantage of the pop in volatility and let you 'call a bottom' because the spread created room for it.

With USO trading $9.33 and IV at 44% the strikes are shown in Figure 10.3.

Strike	Bid	Ask	IV	Delta	Volume	OI
USO Nov18 7.5	0.22	0.27	47.99	16.67	2	912
USO Nov18 8	0.29	0.37	44.71	22.53	70	22746
USO Nov18 8.5	0.51	0.55	45.94	30.89	43	11143
USO Nov18 9	0.71	0.75	44.66	39.30	2056	3337
USO Nov18 9.5	0.93	0.98	43.65	48.20	435	4873

Figure 10.3: USO strikes out of the money.

To pick a bottom, you could set up a 1 by 2 by buying a 9 put for 0.75 and selling two of the 8.5 puts at 0.53 each. With the 0.31 credit taken in (1 put for 0.75 on the 9 strike, versus 2 puts sold at 0.53 on the 8.5 strike), USO could drop to $7.69 before you would be down on the trade.

What makes the trade work? The *high* IV and the extreme price. Traders are often paralyzed by the concept of selling puts on a major market move; a trade like this allows traders to take advantage of that movement. The risk is realized if the timing is wrong.

On the other side, if a stock rallies higher, a front spread can be a great way to fade a strong move up. It is dangerous to sell short calls on a stock that is off to the races, but when a stock rallies and IV does the same, that can signal that the stock price is going to slow down (look at AAPL price and IV in Figure 10.4).

Figure 10.4: Price of APPL and IV of options.

As AAPL broke out in mid-September, IV exploded. As the stock topped out, so did volatility. That is a setup for an amazing front spread. With the stock trading at $113, the structure in October options is shown in Figure 10.5.

OI	Volume	Delta	IV	Bid	Ask	Strike
5271	5804	50.97	18.91	1.80	1.82	AAPL Oct21 113
6619	5177	42.24	18.56	1.32	1.34	AAPL Oct21 114
183398	14961	33.80	18.38	0.94	0.95	AAPL Oct21 115
7727	2631	26.17	18.33	0.66	0.67	AAPL Oct21 116
25230	4220	19.46	18.20	0.45	0.46	AAPL Oct21 117
4327	1156	14.11	18.23	0.30	0.31	AAPL Oct21 118
4345	261	10.18	18.49	0.20	0.21	AAPL Oct21 119
86765	2135	7.25	18.78	0.14	0.15	AAPL Oct21 120
1993	245	5.31	19.31	0.09	0.10	AAPL Oct21 121

Figure 10.5: Grouping of AAPL calls.

You could have bought the 115 calls and sold the 117 calls, paying almost nothing. You would be buying the 115 calls for 0.95 and selling two 117 calls at 0.46 (a net debit of 0.03). In paying 0.03 for the spread, AAPL could run to $118.97 and still make money. If you bought the 115 calls and the underlying rallied, you would have made $10 for every $2 lost on the 117 contract. At expiration, if the 115s were worth 3.97 (with the underlying at $118.97) the 117s would be worth 1.97 each. The trade was up huge dollars, even as the underlying rallied. This is due to the combination of time decay and IV drop.

There are many other reasons to execute a front spread trade. They are excellent spreads for income trading, but executing on the back of a move in volatility makes these spreads more palatable.

Skew

The next key to a front spread is the potential behind a change in skew. The steeper the curvature in the direction of the trade, the more likely that trade is to be successful. Why? Because with a steep skew the trade will be likely to collect a greater credit for the same width of spread. In the example of an AAPL front spread in Figure 10.5, the October 117 calls had 0.03 of vega. What if you had bought the 115 calls for 18.38 volatility and sold 19 volatility instead?

Taking 0.67 (change in vol)*0.03 (vega) = 0.02 of extra premium in each 117 call.

The 117 calls would have a market of 0.46–0.48 or even 0.47–0.48, depending on how tight the market was. That would allow a front spread to collect 4 cents more in the trade at onset relative to what you would expect based on theoretical pricing. Four cents pays the commission in and out of the trade, and gives you an extra few pennies of yield to collect. It makes the trade easier.

You may be able to widen the spread out. While, in the AAPL case, that 1 point in volatility might only increase the credit by 0.04, in SPX as close as a week out, each strike can have vega near 0.50–1.00 per contract, depending on time and placement.

That extra premium allows you to move the front spread an additional $5.00 and receive a similar, if not better, credit. The curvature in the trade makes a huge difference in how you set up the strikes.

While volatility is the key to a good front spread trade, if skew is in the spread's favor, it makes a front spread especially likely to succeed. When skew gets extra steep, that can be a sign that the move is likely to be nearing an end.

The CBOE SKEW index tends to have a positive correlation with the market. When skew gets super steep, it's bullish, and when flat, bearish. With a front spread looking for a turnaround, skew can be the difference between an easy winner and a hard-fought victory.

HV

The final piece to a good front spread is a slowing down of movement. Much like every other short premium trade, a profitable front spread expects movement to slow down (even more so, in many cases, than a condor or butterfly). A slowdown of momentum can be seen when HV drops while volume also drops. Let's look at AAPL again.

Volume (the lighter portion of the price graph in Figure 10.6) peaked with HV (a lagging indicator). One day of falling volume was a dip; 2–3 days of falling volume led to sinking HV.

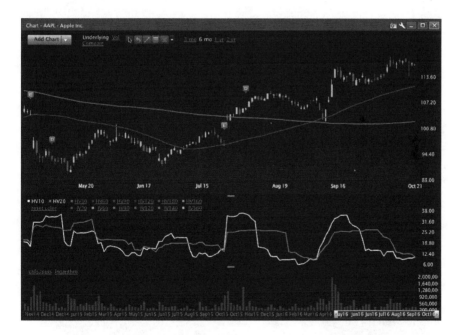

Figure 10.6: The more volatile line is 10 day HV, the smoother line is 20 day HV.

That sinking HV meant that the 'nasty move' was over and a continuing move meant it would slow down. More often than not, this means the smart money is selling their wins to the retail side. If you can set up a front spread near peaks when HV is starting to sink, combined with great IV and skew, the front spread will work.

The Broken Wing Butterfly

What is the difference between a broken wing butterfly and a front spread? Almost nothing. The broken wing buys an extra option away from the two short strikes. This is done for two reasons.

1. Limit margin
2. Limit risk

The trade looks just like a front spread. In AAPL, you could have set up a front spread expiring in three weeks that was long ATM, short about 3% OTM, and long 10% OTM, to reduce the margin on the trade and ensure that you did not 'blow out' if AAPL reversed (see Figure 10.7).

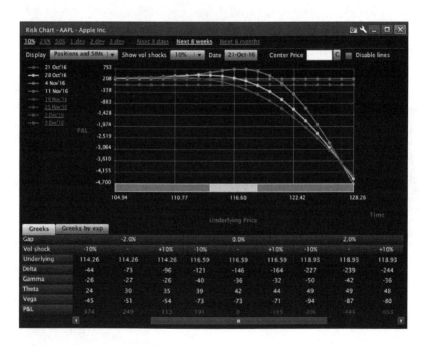

Figure 10.7: The payout on a 115–117 call 1 by 2.

Aside from the reduced credit and limited upside, the two trades were practically identical.

Trade Management

There are two ways to manage these trades: aggressively or passively.

Aggressive Management

A trader typically manages delta of the position on a daily basis. When I was a floor trader, I traded to keep the delta of the position no more than twice my gamma; this allowed the position to move without needing to adjust (especially since adjustments reduce the profitability of a trade). Others kept it 1-to-1 on a daily basis, still others were much closer managers and let delta slip to 2 to 3 times gamma of the position. In managing delta, I used the stock or future, hedging with the underlying.

This method is appropriate if you use margin to trade these positions or trade the pure 1 by 2 positions because it will keep the trade from getting out of hand; no one wants a loss. Managing delta of a 1 by 2 ensures it doesn't explode into an account blowing loser. I suggest going conservative and keeping delta at no more than 1-to-1 against a portfolio position. In Appendix A, managing delta over the course of a few days is explored.

Passive Management

This is more appropriate for the retail trader or those trading broken wing butterflies. In passive management, let the trade sit until the underlying gets to the long strike. Once this occurs, slowly buy close calls or puts from the short strike to reduce delta. In adjusting this way, you will see two things happen to the position. The trade will become net long contracts and the short gamma of the position will drop. As the gamma drops, the pain will be reduced; and if the underlying pops, your long contracts will kick in, allowing you to break even on continued momentum which, given the odds on a 1 by 2, sets up long-term success when these are executed repeatedly. We love these spreads because the odds work well for the consistent trader.

Beginning of Front Spread in TSLA

Let's examine a front spread in TSLA:

At the onset, this is a classic front spread; you buy a near-the-money call and sell 2 OTM calls (see Figure 10.8).

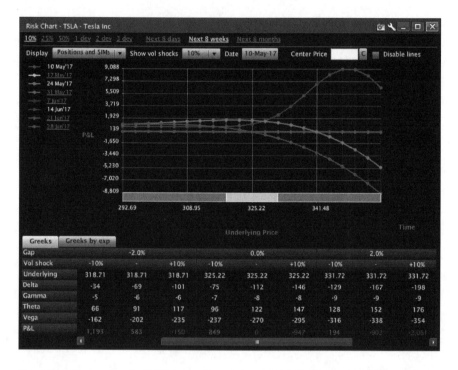

Figure 10.8: You are long in 10 335 June calls and short in 20 350 calls, for a small net credit.

As the stock moves higher, you buy 3 350 calls to hedge off risk. This exploits the upward movement with an increased position on the long side. Figure 10.9 shows a TSLA front spread after a few days pass, managed with more calls.

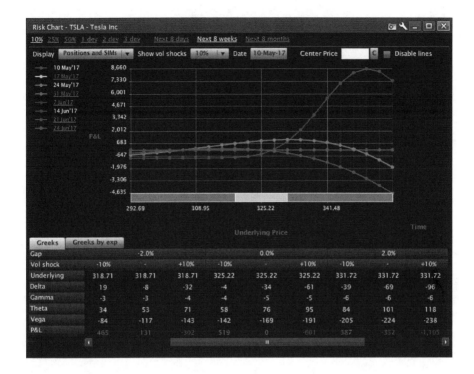

Figure 10.9: The stock moves higher and you buy 3 more calls at the 350 strike.

If you aggressively cover, the underlying will not be a problem. The trade can have a P&L curve much like graph number one, where a strong move puts the trader in real trouble.

At this point, cut the delta in half every time it increases to the point that it 'takes over' the position. If you cut delta in half when delta starts to be the number one concern, you have a chance to make the front spread work. You can do this by buying calls or buying the underlying to handle delta. In the above example, you bought calls. This meant keeping delta in a position that it would not be so high that a move against you would put the entire position in peril. This means keeping delta at two times gamma. You can also look at the P&L of the position to manage risk. Never lose more than you are trying to make—as that becomes in doubt, delta should be cut.

Target Profit

Do not look at the margin unless you are on PM (portfolio margin). The margin associated with front spreads is high relative to risk. I prefer to look at these in terms of how much I am willing to lose, and set my P&L targets there. Thus, if I am willing to lose $500 on a trade, I shoot for $500–1,000 in profit. That is equivalent to selling a 1 by 2 at 0.30 and covering it for a 0.30 credit.

Front Spread checklist:
1. What is the probable direction of the trade?
2. What is the IV?
3. What is the skew?
4. Where is the momentum and HV?
5. What is the target for the trade?

Using this checklist, you can develop a profitable front spread and a set of front spread trading positions.

Broken Wing Butterfly Variation

Returning to the TSLA example, a variant is the broken wing butterfly (as discussed earlier in this chapter). This is a front spread combining one long contract close to the money, with two short contracts out of the money. It is much like a front spread, but your long contract is further away from the two shorts. This reduces margin. The net of the trade produces a credit but limits risk if the underlying keeps moving (see Figure 10.10).

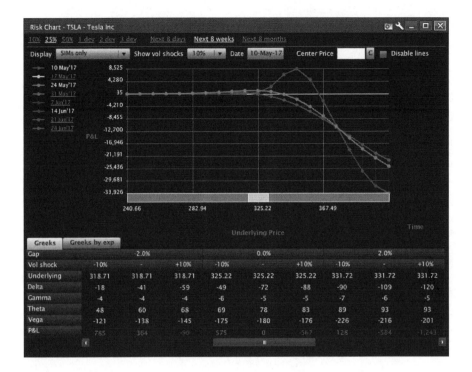

Figure 10.10: The payout on a TSLA broken wing butterfly at onset and expiration.

The chart looks a lot like a front spread, however, margin is reduced because you own an OTM call. Trading a broken wing is almost exactly like trading a front spread. The difference is that as the underlying rallies and you cover, the position loses less. Consider the broken wing butterfly as an alternative to the front spread.

Chapter 11
Calendar Spreads

The *calendar spread* is a trade betting that IV in one month is mispriced against another. While many view calendars as long or short implied volatility trades, in actuality, calendars are a play on the exact opposite. A calendar spread is a play on movement. Compare the long calendar to a short straddle. Figure 11.1 shows a risk chart of a short straddle for the SPX, whereas Figure 11.2 shows a calendar spread for the SPX under the same conditions.

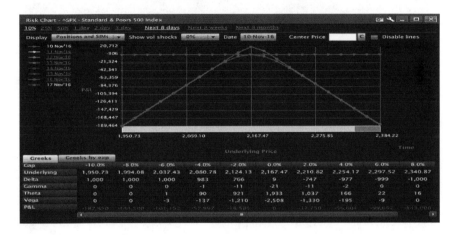

Figure 11.1: A short straddle for SPX.

The only difference between the two is that there is a limit to how much a calendar can lose. On the surface, though, calendar spreads and straddles are in a sense the same trade. The major difference is that owning the back-month contract creates a hedge in the case of a major move and it creates a hedge if and when IV explodes.

https://doi.org/10.1515/9781501505676-011

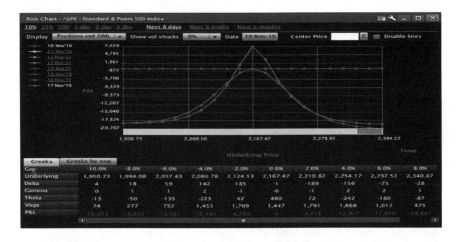

Figure 11.2: The calendar spread under the same conditions for SPX.

Creating a Calendar

A calendar is exposure to *realized volatility*, but with sensitivity to implied volatility rallying. It's a vol swap. You are betting that near-term volatility is too high and long-term volatility is too low. You also believe that the overall perception of volatility is too low, while movement itself is sinking. To say these are complex vehicles is an understatement; however, you can develop a trade with a ton of edge in it and have a hard time losing while enjoying huge upside potential. Here are the steps to developing a good calendar spread.

1. Evaluate overall implied volatility
2. Evaluate term structure
3. Evaluate event risk
4. Evaluate realized volatility
5. Evaluate the market trend
6. Choose the right strikes
7. Execute the trade
8. Manage the trade
9. Exit

Evaluate Overall Implied Volatility

Calendars do best when they are executed in a low implied volatility environment. Like all purchases, the lower the price, the better. In addition to a lower price, since IV is mean reverting both within and between zones, buying calendars when volatility is cheap will lead to trades with higher odds of success. The next chart in Figure 11.3 is VXAPL.

Figure 11.3: The above chart is of VXAPL, the VIX of AAPL options.

In July and August, IV of AAPL options was cheap (compared with past movement)—at levels where you should buy. IV was low over this period. AAPL prices in August versus September for an option with 30 days to expire reveal more. Figure 11.4 shows August 9th options:

OI	Volume	Delta	IV	Bid	Ask	Strike	Bid	Ask	IV	Delta	Volume	OI
1492	62	64.27	17.31	3.20	3.30	AAPL(W) Sep09 107	1.34	1.37	17.37	35.72	114	305
3284	2115	57.22	17.25	2.60	2.65	AAPL(W) Sep09 108	1.72	1.76	17.10	42.68	76	114
918	554	49.93	17.06	2.07	2.11	AAPL(W) Sep09 109	2.19	2.22	17.02	50.02	78	69
5481	2202	42.60	16.96	1.61	1.65	AAPL(W) Sep09 110	2.72	2.77	16.91	57.37	9	85

Figure 11.4: AAPL options with 30 days to expire—from August 9 to September 9.

In the montage above the ATM options (using the offer price) cost about 2.4% of the value of the underlying stock (2.1/109 = 1.92%). Options with 30 days remaining until September expiration are shown in Figure 11.5.

OI	Volume	Delta	IV	Bid	Ask	Strike	Bid	Ask	IV	Delta	Volume	OI
1398	914	61.57	21.52	3.70	3.85	AAPL(W) Oct14 110	1.87	1.92	21.23	38.31	2623	102
732	1996	55.92	21.22	3.10	3.25	AAPL(W) Oct14 111	2.27	2.33	21.09	44.06	1467	85
1254	1165	50.04	21.03	2.61	2.67	AAPL(W) Oct14 112	2.74	2.79	20.94	49.97	268	13
663	870	44.14	20.93	2.15	2.20	AAPL(W) Oct14 113	3.25	3.35	20.80	55.91	223	24

Figure 11.5: AAPL options with about 30 days to expire, September 14 to October 14.

The ATM options cost about 2.4% of the value of the stock (2.65/112 = .0237). That is no small difference in straddle price for a stock costing $100.00 per share. .50 in a straddle is a big change in straddle price; now let's think about how that might affect much large stock and index options In the SPX or NDX indexes with values in the thousands, instead of 0.50 a spread in the bid-ask in index options can be worth 5.0–6.5 dollars per contract or more. That is not a small dollar amount in an option spread. Most traders in index options are only trying to make 1.00 to 2.00 on the entire trade. Thus, small changes in IV can dramatically change the cost of the straddle and will mean the difference between a trade with high odds and a trade likely to lose.

When VXAPL is low, calendar spreads are cheaper, making them potent. However, overall low IV is not the only way price is determined. The second (and almost as important) piece of overall pricing is term structure.

Evaluate Term Structure

The next key to a calendar is the relationship between contract months; the IV of one week or month against another. It's not enough to have low volatility if the option being sold is also too cheap. When IV is low, term structure tends to steepen, just like a VIX futures curve. Vol is low in the near-term contract, but gets progressively higher with each week and month. Because IV is low, the assumption that IVs will revert higher pulls the curve. When it's low, traders look for a quicker and slightly stronger reversion; however, unlike the VIX futures curve, the structure is far more inefficient. Vol doesn't move as smoothly across contracts in individual months among index options, especially with daily and weekly options. It is even less efficient in equity options, where one trade can throw off the entire volatility curve in one month relative to all the other months. Figure 11.6 is a chart of options on AAPL.

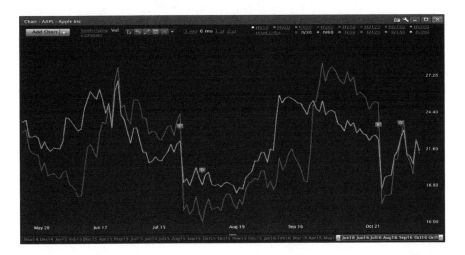

Figure 11.6: AAPL options IV.

Even when IV is low, spreads between the 30 and 60 day IV widen and tighten over time. When IVs tighten and IV is low, calendars can work and work quickly. However, with weekly and daily options now available, it's not enough to look at simple vol charts. You need to study aggregate vol. Look at the weeks in Figure 11.7 to determine which contracts can be bought or sold.

Expiry	Nov18	Nov25(W)	Dec02(W)	Dec09(W)	Dec16	Dec23(W)	Dec30(W)	Jan20'17	Feb17'17	Mar17'17
Sigma	22.76	20.57	20.89	20.94	21.91	21.38	21.15	21.81	24.54	23.92
Sigma Chg	-3.47	-2.29	-1.64	-1.32	-1.07	-0.96	-0.86	-0.58	-0.35	-0.26

Figure 11.7: The volatility of AAPL options over several expirations.

You could have bought the December 30 contract and sold the December 2 or December 9 contract for even volatility. You could get a credit selling the December 16 against the December 30, but there might be a reason not to, as explained in the next paragraph.

Evaluate Event Risk

In Figure 11.7, December 16 seemed to have a much higher IV than the contracts in front of and behind it. Why? If you don't review event risk, you would overlook the fact that December 16 was the week of a major FOMC (Federal Open Market

Committee) meeting. Traders believed that the FOMC might raise rates in December, but the result was not certain at the time. Because of this belief, IVs were high across the board in all major stocks and indexes for the December 16 contract. This means that IV term structure likely did not have an edge around that contract. Unless you were willing to hold through the Fed meeting, there was no edge in being short the December 16 contract. Given our belief in not trading events, the high IV amounts to no theoretical edge. Thus, you would be better off taking a small negative vol trade selling December 2 and buying December 30 than doing a trade around December 16. If you are looking for edge, event risk is not the way to trade.

Evaluate Realized Volatility

While overall IV and term structure are the primary keys to trading calendars, also recognize the movement of the underlying. If the underlying is moving a lot, a calendar will lose. Thus, while you should look at the IVs, you also need to examine HV movement (see Figure 11.8).

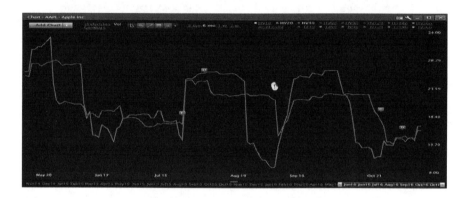

Figure 11.8: 20 and 30 day HV in AAPL.

Like a straddle, a calendar wants the underlying to sit; so look for periods where movement is starting to fall. In August, you could have set up a trade that bought cheap volatility just as movement stopped—a great time to execute a trade. Alternatively, movement is mean reverting, so the times where movement was at its lowest could line up with low volatility. Trade into sinking movement, *not* bottoming out movement. Look at movement *with* IV in SPX in Figure 11.9.

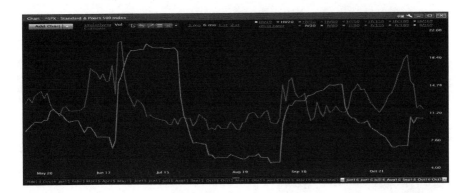

Figure 11.9: 20 day HV and 30 day IV in SPX.

The time to execute a calendar was in late July when HV was dropping and IV was low. At the end of August, HV was bottoming and vol was low, but then HV started to move again. It is important to pay attention not to where HV is, but the direction of movement. If HV is falling and is in the toilet, that could be a great time to execute a calendar. If HV and IV are both low, that might seem like a great spread, but might not have as much edge in the trade.

Choose the Right Strikes

Don't ignore strike-to-strike volatility—how one strike's IV is priced against that of another strike. Within a month, each strike has its own volatility and that can be expensive or cheap. Examining standard term structure provides insight into where volatility is currently; in order to optimize a trade, review each strike to find the right price. Look at the December 9 contract and December 30 contract in AAPL around the ATM strikes as shown in Figure 11.10.

Expiry	Nov18	Nov25(W)	Dec02(W)	Dec09(W)	Dec16	Dec23(W)	Dec30(W)	Jan20'17	Feb17'17	Mar17'17
Sigma	22.76	20.57	20.89	20.94	21.91	21.38	21.15	21.81	24.54	23.92
Sigma Chg	-3.47	-2.29	-1.64	-1.32	-1.07	-0.96	-0.86	-0.58	-0.35	-0.26

Strike	Last	PnL	Pos	SIM	Bid	Thec	Ask	Vol
AAPL(W) Dec09 107	2.07				1.83	1.88	1.93	21.90
AAPL(W) Dec09 108	2.25				2.23	2.28	2.34	21.50
AAPL(W) Dec09 109	2.75				2.69	2.75	2.81	21.07
AAPL(W) Dec09 110	3.23				3.20	3.30	3.40	20.83

Strike	Last	PnL	Pos	SIM	Bid	Thec	Ask	Vol
AAPL(W) Dec30 107	2.75				2.58	2.66	2.74	21.55
AAPL(W) Dec30 108	3.22				3.00	3.10	3.20	21.36
AAPL(W) Dec30 109	3.75				3.45	3.52	3.60	20.77
AAPL(W) Dec30 110	4.37				3.95	4.05	4.15	20.52

Figure 11.10: Strike prices in AAPL in options in the December 9 and December 30 contracts.

The spread between the different strikes varies from strike to strike. The 107s have a vol spread of 0.35 (21.9 less 21.55), the 108s are 0.14, the 109s are 0.30 and the 110s are 0.31.

Based on the spreads, there is more potential in trading the 108 calendar with its tighter spreads than the other contracts. If you are setting up an ATM calendar, the 108s appear to be the strike to trade as the IV spread is less than half of the surrounding strikes. While 0.14 to 0.3 might not seem like much based on the net vega of the spread, which is about 4 cents in the calendar, executing the 108 would produce an extra 0.01 in the calendar. A penny is equal to the commission on the trade.

If you are able to trade commission-free, how much more would you make in a year? While you can't trade commission-free, you can create enough edge in a trade to negate its cost.

Execute the Trade

If you put on a calendar and then the underlying moves (unless the move is a crazy hard move), given the edge executed in the trade, the trade should be near break-even or only slightly down. Practice closing these trades almost immediately. A well-executed calendar should make money in a few days. If it doesn't, or starts losing money, there might not have been nearly as much edge, or the edge could lose. Closing trades with edge that lose, quickly, and then making money on the winners should result in more profits than losses.

An alternative to this management tactic is to add a calendar in the direction of movement. This is a more nuanced approach to management, and requires conditions the trader liked about the first calendar to still be in effect, thus the calendar would have an edge to it. If you do this, you will end up with a double calendar that will be around the current price. However, you still need to have great calendar trading conditions. In this scenario, you sell a calendar one strike beyond where the underlying is currently trading; thus, if you executed an AAPL 150 calendar initially, and the stock ran to 155, you would then add a calendar at the 157.5 or 160 strike (see Figure 11.11).

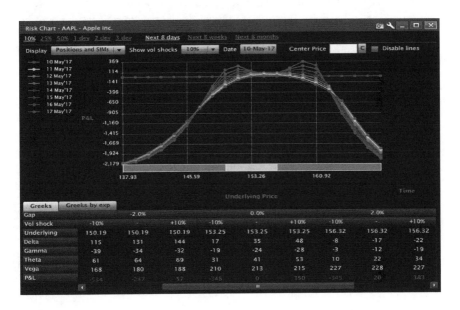

Figure 11.11: Adding subsequent calendars.

The underlying is now surrounded by calendar spreads. If the underlying sits, you will make money as time passes and if IV runs higher. If the things that make a calendar not work continue to happen, you will lose more. This is why, when the conditions for a calendar are no longer present on the initial spread, you should kill the trade.

Manage the Trade

With calendar spreads traded for edge, we believe in the simple approach to adjusting. Each trade should have edge. We look for a simple approach to calendar management.

Exit

When managing a calendar, you should be going for about 10–15% of the margin, while looking to lose less than 5%. If this is done over time, calendar trading should produce net overall profits. The absolute max loss on a calendar should be about what you are trying to make in profit. The key is the edge though. If you trade these with edge over time, calendars will win.

Part III: **Global Risk**

Chapter 12
How a Market Maker Trades

How do market makers trade? There are two answers, a general approach and a "manage the book" approach. At the onset, how a trader acts is what builds the book. Market makers would rather be involved in trading, not in building the book. This is a primary driver in option pricing; market makers dislike carrying positions.

Market Making

The story of market making begins with middlemen. They do one thing: manage demand, regardless of their actual jobs. Middlemen buy fish from fishermen, then sell them at the wharf. Middlemen buy furniture, then sell it to office managers when they need to furnish their offices. Middlemen are some of the biggest companies in the world. Walmart is the world's largest middleman.

With stocks, middlemen take a different name: market maker. In a perfect world, the market would be able to match buyers to sellers exactly. This does happen every now and then, but most of the time someone has to buy an unwanted stock, or sell a wanted stock to an individual and hold the opposite position for a period of time. Here is how stock market making works:

– A market maker presents a market on XYZ currently trading at $100.00
– The bid is $99.95 for 1,000 shares and the offer is $100.05
– The offer trades as the underlying prints (sells at) $100.05
– The market after the trade is: The bid is $100.00 for 1,000 shares and the offer is $100.05
– The bid trades $100.00. The market maker makes $100.05 – 100, netting $0.05 on 1,000 shares, or $50.00

Fifteen years ago, that was the model on a few hundred million shares a day. Now that there a billion shares a day, spreads have tightened to 0.02 wide for active stocks and 0.05 wide for less liquid stocks. The 'trade by appointment' stocks still can have spread-widths of 0.20 or more. In a given day, a firm can make good money simply buying stock, holding it for a few seconds, and then selling it to someone else.

Why do market makers make money? Because they are willing to hold a position for a short period of time. However, because market makers don't want to hold a position, markets move. This movement is the risk the market maker takes.

https://doi.org/10.1515/9781501505676-012

Prints can go in stocks when the underlying moves. For example, consider the intra-day tick chart of NDX in Figure 12.1.

Figure 12.1: A daily tick chart of the NDX.

From 10:30 AM to 12:00 PM the stock went straight up, yet the market maker had to take the risk of being short the NDX over that brief time. For this reason, market makers are able to trade on the bid/offer spread. In the end, they do not make $50 dollars per trade or even $20; it ends up amounting to less than $1.00 per trade. With dynamic hedging (hedging as the delta moves), direction should not be important as hedging takes directional moves out of the equation (except for gaps).

While the above is similar to option market making, it is not exactly the same. A stock market maker needs to make markets in one instrument, the stock. A market maker in options needs to make markets in hundreds of strikes, all of which move with the underlying. While a market maker could try to make markets on each individual case, given the scope of the job and the correlated relationship of each contract, option market makers have to move all options when a single option trades.

Option traders, in order to manage the entire curve, need to trade volatility. Look at the vol chart of AAPL in Figure 12.2.

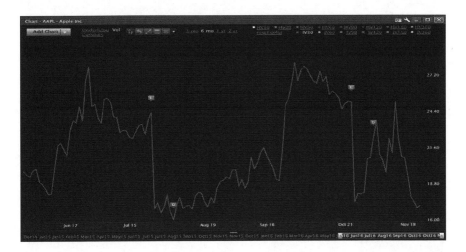

Figure 12.2: A 30 day vol chart of AAPL options.

Much like a stock price, option volatility moves around on a daily basis and moment to moment. This point is made in Figure 12.3.

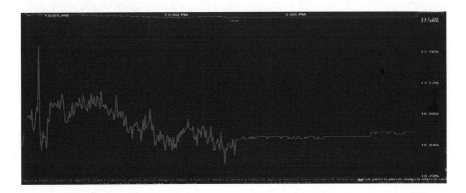

Figure 12.3: A daily tick chart for AAPL options.

At any given time, regardless of the movement in the stock, the vol price is based on what traders buy and sell. Market makers trade volatility on option prices. They hedge off directional risk when they trade and hedge delta as the underlying moves. A trader might set his fair value volatility at 40: for example, you might set your vols based on 39 bid and 41 offer.

When you trade an option, regardless of the strike, it is going to move volatility. Whether you buy an out-of-the-money option or an in-the-money option, downside or upside, volatility is going to move. Because you bought an option, the new vol levels may move to 40 bid and 42 offer. While this example is more extreme than movement most of the time, it's indicative of how markets are made by market makers.

The market makers do not want to hold too strong a position one way or the other. By moving markets based on vol, you avoid establishing too large of a position. If vols get too high, someone, likely a professional customer, will sell the overpriced volatility back to the market maker. The market maker will have very little position open, and vol pricing will be near equilibrium.

The Trader

What does this have to do with the retail or 'prop' trader? The above approach applies to those *producing* trades. One of the major mistakes retail traders make is over-playing their hand. By this I mean that traders tend to sell or buy too much. Thus, you should approach position building much like a market maker; you don't wait for the trade to come to you, but allow your trades to determine the next trade increment. The first trade shouldn't be the biggest.

The most powerful weapon you have is your ability to initiate a trade, or *not* initiate it. When trading, you will tend to think it is important to develop a management system. A numbers system can work (this is something we work on with people at Option Pit) or it can be some other approach. We like our students to rank each trade on a scale from 1 to 5. The higher the number, the more they pay to remove risk. This way, we rank the likelihood of success on a trade. If a trade is good, it should demand less capital. The equation is direct: by ranking your trade based on risk, you identify an appropriate level of risk you are willing to take. Too many traders fail to understand this and end up losing money because they lacked a rating system.

The first key to portfolio building is to develop a rating system for this purpose. How good is this trade? If it's a great trade, you might apply a rating of a 7 or 8 on a scale of 1 to 10. If the trade isn't that great, you might apply 5. If the trade is below 5, don't even bother. This is something traders do all the time. Market makers have an advantage: They see orders come in, and do not generate them. The fact that orders have to be generated by upstairs traders and the public makes the process of rating trades that much more important. As you create the trade, you are not getting the bid-ask spread. The only value the upstairs trader has is the edge generated by the trade. Prop desk and major upstairs traders likely go through this process in their heads as well. We think the retail public (which does not have the luxury of managing a multi-million dollar book) needs, at the onset, to use a system of rating each trade.

Here are the steps for rating a trade:

Step 1

Establish fair value of a given trade. This may be a credit received, given the risk, or it may be a value above a theoretical value. Newer traders tend to go with the former and more experienced traders will go with the latter. For our assumptions, this example is the former. The fair value should be set for each trade, and really for each product (which really means the volatility of the underlying). Time spreads and similar trades are a little more complicated as it's the vol spread that sets the edge, but all things being equal, it's not that different from buying or selling a single option.

Step 2

What is the maximum capital to allocate to a trade? If a trade is just okay, you might be willing to place 2% of your portfolio at risk. If a trade is a home run, you might be willing to put 5% toward the trade. Even the absolute home run percentage should be less than the maximum you are willing to apply toward a trade. If we have one rule it is, "always be able to trade." Thus, while a single position should never take more than 10% of your portfolio, it should not meet the maximum and should be limited, probably to about 5% maximum.

Step 3

Slowly build a book. One of the mistakes retail traders make is the failure to let the right trade come to them. While you have to press the buy or sell button, you do not have to do it on any specific date or time. Traders that take the time to let a good trade "show up" (and by that, I mean set criteria, stick to them, and wait for the right trade) will be more successful than those traders that wing it. The key is that as the book builds, the rating system changes. While at the onset you might be willing to trade a 3 out of 5, after one trade, the next trade needs to be a 4, and then a 5 after that. The next trade, if it's not a 5, needs to be skipped. In fact, if an offer on the other side of the current position comes in near a 3, you might be willing to take the trade if you have sold recently at 5.

While you rate each trade, in the end, you look at the portfolio as a whole. We are going to look at a portfolio in the next section and how it might be built in a single day. We discuss managing the portfolio as a whole in the next two chapters.

Step 4

Unwind the book. Much like putting on a trade, take trades off in waves. If the trade makes the profit target quickly and you only have one trade on, the plan becomes easy; close the trade. If you have many trades on, it is more convoluted. This is where profit targets for every trade matter. The following is an example of how a basic portfolio might trade condors.

Using the Option Pit Method to build a portfolio of trades:
Day 1: Sell a condor with a rating 3: 2%
Day 2: Sell a condor with a rating 4: 2%
Day 3: Sell a condor with a rating 5: 4%
Day 4: Sell a condor with a rating 5: 2%

Even though you saw a rating of 5 on day 4, you only sold 2%; this is because the condor as a whole had allocated 10% of the portfolio's risk. Thus, even though it was better than the day 1 trade, it went at the same level. You should not stop yourself from being able to trade by trading too much at one time. This is the key to the day 4 sale level.

Now looking at a larger portfolio, the tricky part is understanding that each trade adds on to the next. A trade done is additive to the entirety of the portfolio:
Day 1: Sell a condor with a rating 3: 2%
Day 2: Sell an iron butterfly with a rating 5: 5%
Day 3: Buy a straddle with a rating 3: 2%
Day 4: Sell an iron butterfly with a rating 5: 5%
Day 5: Buy a straddle with a rating 3: 4%

Even though the trades are all different, they offset to some degree. Yet this does not negate the fact that each trade does not exceed 5%. If you do too much of the same thing, you have to stop trading. Build a portfolio in which you understand what each trade means to the overall picture. You should build, in our opinion, a spreadsheet that helps you keeps track.

Setting numbers to every trade is part of your retail trader training. It transforms how you look at the Greeks and risk into a skill. To manage a book, you need to be able to weight and understand the Greeks. To do that you need to use weighted Greeks, the right forms of vega, and total delta management.

Chapter 13
Portfolio Greeks

Traders have a choice to look at each trade individually, or as a whole. Looking at the investment portfolio as a whole is usually the more profitable choice, but requires an understanding of how the Greeks operate and how to evaluate aggregate Greeks. This chapter discusses how portfolio Greeks add up, and the proper calculation of vega.

Delta

All deltas are not the same. This is because delta is not weighted. You can be long 100 deltas of AAPL and long 100 deltas of Bank of America (BA), yet the exposure is different because of the price and volatility of each stock. This is where the concept of beta weighting comes into play. Beta weighting a portfolio to a base index is key. This is a practice engaged in by many trading firms, including some of the largest market making firms in the world. So how *do* you beta weight?

The first step is to pick the right index to beta weight a portfolio against. Most active traders' portfolios are best weighted to the S&P 500. The SPX has the most active futures and most traders do not specialize in only one sector. The alternative is to beta weight to a different index, potentially the NDX or RUT; the NDX (NASDAQ-100 Index) is a good choice if you trade a lot of the major tech stocks, or you can choose RUT (Russell 2000 Index) if you specialize in small cap names. If you have a smaller portfolio, you could weight to the ETF of the index instead of the index (SPY, QQQ, or IWM). There are brokerage platforms that have beta weighting already programmed and others that do not. However, the concept is the same.

https://doi.org/10.1515/9781501505676-013

BETA WEIGHTING

Divide the price of the underlying by the price of the beta index to get a relative ratio taking the stock's price into consideration; then multiply by the beta of the underlying to the index to get a per share ratio that can be used to compare to other stocks.

Thus, for a stock worth $110 dollars per share versus the S&P 500 with an index price of $2,200, 100 deltas (for 100 shares) would become:

100 * 110/2200 = 5.0 (the relative ratio)

Next, multiply by the beta of the underlying to the S&P 500. If the beta is 0.96:

5.0 * 0.96 = 4.8

Thus, the beta weighted delta of AAPL would become 4.8.

Thus, for every 100 shares of stock, if a trader is long, it contributes 4.8 deltas to an S&P 500 weighted index.

It is not hard to find beta weighting based on historical deltas; it simply involves comparing historical volatility of the underlying to the weighted index. By beta weighting, you are able to gauge the exposure of a portfolio due to a move in a major index like the S&P 500.

Gamma

The effect of beta weighting on gamma is much the same as the effect beta weighting has on delta. Because gamma is how the delta changes with a one point move, when a portfolio is beta weighted gamma, it will also convert and can be calculated in similar fashion.

Change gamma by the same adjustment made to delta. Thus, a stock with delta of 110 and gamma of 100 would see its gamma converted, relative to the SPX, by the same effect: 100 deltas convert to 4.8 deltas and has a beta multiplier of .048. Applying this to gamma converts 100 gamma to a gamma of 4.8 as well.

Essentially, to convert gamma:
1. Calculate the delta beta weighted conversion ratio
2. Multiply this number by the gamma

While not exact, this will be better than a back of the envelope conversion for those using a spreadsheet to calculate a beta weighted portfolio.

Theta and Vega

Unlike delta and gamma when beta weighting, theta and vega are already weighted.

Theta

Theta represents the amount a position costs or produces with a daily passage of time. Because this number is derived from premium paid or collected, it is already weighted if you sell premium at the same delta. A single contract sold at 3.00 with 32 days to expire will, if it goes out worthless, produce $300 of decay and a similar theta number to a contract with delta sold at 0.30 10 times. It does not matter if it was SPX or a $30 stock; $300 of premium at a given delta sold in SPX will have a similar rate of decay (theta) compared to the same amount of premium sold in a $150 stockl. An example can be seen in the AAPL options vs. SPX options in Figures 13.1 and 13.2.

The two options, with similar expirations and deltas have the same amount of theta.

Figure 13.1: Short 1 SPX 15 delta call at a 15 delta

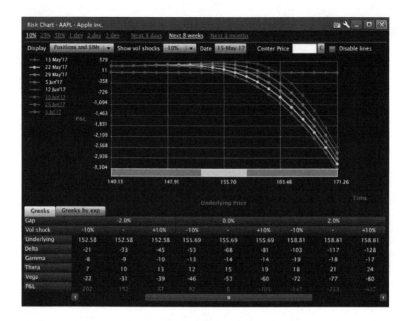

Figure 13.2: Short 6 AAPL options with 32 days decay at a 17 delta.

In Figures 13.1 and 13.2, the two sales collected similar premium, while the AAPL options produced slightly less theta (the result of a slightly higher delta); the two options produced similar risk, and more importantly, similar theta levels.

Vega

Much like theta, vega is derived from premium collected. In its raw form, vega is already weighted. 1000 vega in AAPL is the same, in raw terms, as 1000 vega in SPX; although the former would need more contracts to create that much volatility exposure. The more premium, the more vol exposure, regardless of price. However, a couple attributes of vega take the analysis a step further. For example, how do you analyze volatility?

Weighted Vega

Vega has a gamma to it, in that as the underlying moves, vega also changes. The closer to expiration, the more the volatility of the option. This can be seen in the price action of VIX futures. While every VIX future represents 1000 vega notionally, in actuality they do not act that way. A near-dated VIX future will have much lower implied volatility than a long-dated VIX future. Figure 13.3 shows a future with X days to expire that has much lower implied volatility than a longer-dated vol future. March is lower than April and April is lower than May, etc.

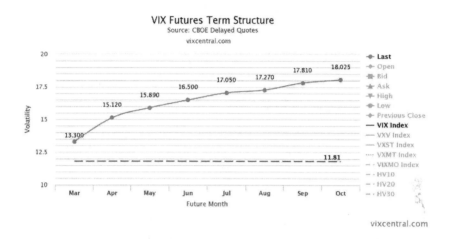

Figure 13.3: VIX Futures term structure

However, that is not the whole story. Because of the near dated nature of short term futures, they have a higher actual volatility (vol of vol) than longer dated futures. A move in VIX will cause near-dated futures to move more than long-dated futures. Take a look at how futures reacted to the French elections of 2017 (Figure 13.4). As the election got closer, VIX rallied, but the VIX futures did not move in unison; near-dated futures rallied harder over the 2 weeks heading into the election than long-dated futures:

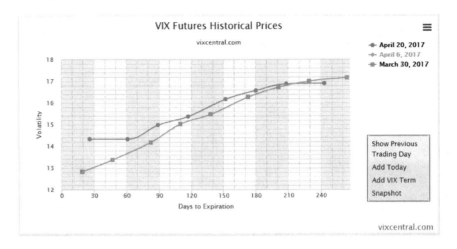

Figure 13.4: Futures Reaction after the French election

Futures with less time to expire moved at a much greater relative speed than long-dated futures and, in some cases, long futures didn't move at all.

Because near-dated volatility is so much more active than long-dated volatility, it becomes important to take this movement into account. Traders generally weight the volatility of their portfolio. By weighting a portfolio, you are able to give more emphasis to volatility in near-dated options than premium held in longer-dated options. There are several ways to calculate weighted vega.

Professional shops run correlation by days to expirations. This means that a professional group has run the correlation of volatility of an option within a single name or index that has 20 days to expiration against how its vol moves against options with expirations from one day to well over a year to expiration. These correlations probably are too much work for an independent managing a small book.

For the independent trader, it makes more sense to use a simple squaring function to calculate weighted vega. To calculate weighted vega, first come up with a base number of days to expiration, a simple standard duration of the portfolio. To do this, take the square root of the standard days to expiration over the days to contract expiration. Thus:

1000 vega with 60 days to expire with a standard duration of 30 days would have a weighted vega of:

1000 * SQRT(30/60)

which becomes:
1000 * 0.707 or a weighted vega of 707.

With a weighed vega of 707, I should expect to make about 0.70 on the dollar relative to my raw vega in the event that volatility increases. Thus, while in theory I am long 1000 vega, if the VIX moves up 1 point, I am likely only to make 707 dollars. This is important because if I have a vol spread long, a short in a near-dated month and long in a further dated month, I am not going to make money on a movement in volatility created by the overall market (something like a market sell off) the way I am expecting. If I am counting on vega to produce profit against the losses in being short gamma on a calendar spread, and if I only looked at raw vega, I am not going to get the results I want.

Using weighted vega will give a portfolio manager a better idea of how the portfolio will perform in a VIX spike than will raw vega alone. Weighted vega is a huge step toward portfolio management, but does not answer the vega question entirely. The next step is to use vol vega.

Vol Vega

Vol vega is a concept I learned at Group One Trading. I had to ask current CEO Jon Kinahan (at the time, head of training and head trader) what it was. He described it this way:

"If you own 1000 vega of a biotech, it is not the same as owning 1000 vega in an industrial. Vol vega adjusts for it."

He then walked through the calculation. Vol vega multiplies how much more volatility the underlying has than the base index has. Thus, if I am long 1000 vega in SPX and at the same time long 1000 vega in AMGN, vol vega adjusts for the differences in the stock's volatility. So if AMGN is two times as volatile as the SPX, SPX would have a vol vega of 1000 and AMGN would have a vol vega of 2000.

Vol vega is one of the most important calculations for anyone trading a wide range of stocks and indexes. It allows you to piece together what your real vol exposure is in the event that volatilities start to move, so that you are prepared for how dramatically the individual components may start to move.

Additionally, and this is the far more important case for vol vega, it is *great* for volatility pair traders (traders that sell volatility in one stock, or month, against another). Imagine I am trying to set up a pair trade between XLF (the Financial Select Sector Spyder Fund) and IBB (a biotech ETF)—yes I know there would never be a pair trade here that is why I used these two. While the two are both index ETFs, they are in very different sectors. If I buy 1000 vega in XLF because I think the vol is cheap, and sell 1000 vega in IBB because I think the vol is too expensive, even if I am right I might not win on volatility because IBB vol can move so much more. Using vol vega allows you to put a vol pair trade together that will make money because of volatility.

As an example, suppose XLF has volatility of 19. IBB has volatility of 27. If volatility increases by 10% in IBB and 15% in XLF, if I am long 1000 vega in both do I actually win?

In IBB, I would lose:

1000 * (27 * 0.10), or 2700

In XLF, I would make:

1000 * (19 * 0.15), or 2850

$150, not bad for a vol trade. But when you consider the capital involved, there were likely better trades. Next, adjust for vol vega.

27/19 is 1.42. Thus, if I traded on vol vega terms, I would go long 1400 vega in XLF for every 1000 vega in IBB. Thus my vega trade would look like this:

1000* (27 * 0.1), or 2700

versus

1400 * (19 * 0.15), or 3060

The end result is more than double the P&L. That is how strong vol vega is in a volatility pair trade.

Managing a Book

Now that we dug into the how to actually value a book of trades, how should you manage the book? It's easy. Manage each trade individually. This make sense in particular if you are carrying fewer than 10 positions. However, when deciding to add to a book, you need to look at net Greeks to develop a portfolio. In the last chapter, we discussed ranking your trades based on the positions carried. In setting up a book to be beta weighted, vega weighted, and with some touch of vol vega, you can rank each trade against the whole portfolio.

Look at each trade on its own merits; if it is a good trade it should be considered, but once you have established positions on more than a few stocks and indexes, you need to start rating trades against the book. If the book is short gamma and short vega, you should be actively trying to find trades that are opposite the existing position. It's easier to evaluate the value of the trade against a book if you are weighting properly.

Weighting will allow you to trade smaller or larger depending on the circumstances of the portfolio. For a portfolio after weighting, you should know which way you are leaning in buying or selling. If you have a clear idea of the net of your portfolio, you can set up a hedge based on movement.

The final attribute of portfolio management is how to manage severe global risk. You can set up a constant hedge or you can engage in crisis alpha management. *Crisis alpha* is a system of going for volatility when it is needed and ignoring it when its unneeded. This is the topic of the next chapter.

Chapter 14
Crisis Alpha

Chapter 14 was written by my good friends Mike and Matt Thompson of Typhon Capital Management. I asked them to write this chapter because while I understand how the process works, they run a fund that engages in the practice. Their domain knowledge exceeds mine and brings more value to you.

* * *

Crisis alpha is a relatively new label in the financial industry used to describe investment strategies designed to generate positive returns during equity market panics. Crisis alpha strategies can range from short-focused hedge funds and trend-following CTAs, to specialized "Black Swan" tail risk protection products. This chapter focuses on generating crisis alpha using VIX futures and options.

Like any insurance product, VIX derivatives have a cost associated with their use. When using these products, seekers of crisis alpha must be cognizant of the cost, which can be substantial, while the equity markets are not experiencing a shock. If not properly managed, accumulated losses from 'always on' protection in VIX can easily outweigh the benefits delivered during the next equity dislocation. It is one thing to deliver alpha during a crisis, but if the overall costs outweigh the benefits, the position may not make sense for an investor's portfolio.

Defining a Market Crisis

Distinct from a run-of-the-mill correction, a "crisis" in markets is a prolonged period of widespread re-pricing of risk assets, usually in response to a macroeconomic shock. In a true crisis, though the initial shock often originates in a specific asset class, its effects often propagate to other assets and may continue reverberating for weeks or months as the markets are waiting for the next shoe to drop. As this process unfolds, cross-asset correlations often rise to near 100%, effectively negating any diversification benefits and increasing demand for near-term options-based protection. This sharp shift in demand results in increased near-term implied volatility relative to medium and long-term measures, eventually inverting the VIX term structure, a condition known in the futures markets as *backwardation*.

Graphically, this is represented as a downward-sloping line connecting short-term implied volatility measures such as the VIX index (30-day S&P 500

https://doi.org/10.1515/9781501505676-014

implied volatility) with the various maturities of VIX futures (1 – 8 month forward VIX) as shown in Figure 14.1.

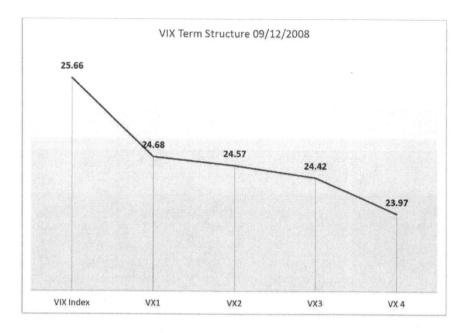

Figure 14.1: Inverted VIX term structure on 9/12/08, the Friday prior to LEH bankruptcy.

Lehman Brothers Bankruptcy

Perhaps the 'gold standard' for an acute market crisis was the period beginning with the bankruptcy of Lehman Brothers on September 15, 2008. Though the initial shock was felt in the financial sector of U.S. equities, it quickly spread into the short-term fixed income (commercial paper) market, causing a 'run' on money market funds that further exacerbated pressure on the balance sheets of large financials, eventually causing the near-collapse of AIG and many of its counterparties over the ensuing weeks.

Importantly, the VIX term structure inverted *before* the crisis began and remained inverted throughout the turbulence of the following weeks (as shown in Figure 14.2). This behavior is distinct from a singular event-driven spike in volatility which is defined by a flattening or brief inversion of the term structure, followed by a quick resolution as the event passes and hedges unwind.

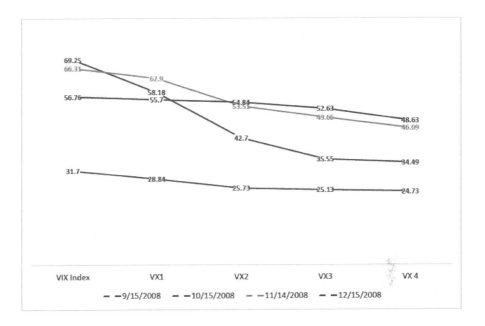

Figure 14.2: VIX term structure evolution, Fall 2008.

VIX Term Structure Determines 'Value' for VIX Derivatives

When it comes to VIX derivatives, the self-evident 'buy low, sell high' rule becomes more complicated. Since they settle to an index which cannot be owned or replicated, VIX futures are a pure 'expectations' market. As such, they trade with a *volatility risk premium* (VRP) not present in most other markets.

VRP is represented by the slope of the VIX term structure. When markets are calm and the VIX index is low, it is common to see a steeply upward-sloping curve that signals high VRP embedded in each VIX future. This becomes hugely impactful for long positions in VIX futures or associated VIX calls which pay this premium *on top of* the typical theta in an option or implied interest rate in a future. Since their introduction in March 2004, the median price difference between the second and first VIX future is approximately 8% per month. In other words, the market assigns (and long VIX positions pay) an 8% premium for the roughly 30-day period between those two expirations (see Figure 14.3).

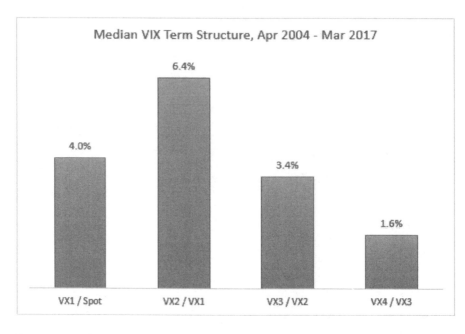

Figure 14.3: Median VIX term structure, April 2004–March 2017.

Factoring in this additional cost sets up the somewhat strange situation where the curve shape can render a long VIX position 'cheap' with the VIX near 20 and 'expensive' with the VIX near 13, confounding the "buy low, sell high" crowd focused solely on the VIX index level. Perhaps nowhere is this phenomenon more apparent than in the $1B iPath S&P 500 Short Term VIX Futures ETN, ticker VXX. VXX is designed to track a constant 30-day maturity VIX future, which means constant exposure to VRP. As shown in Figure 14.4, VXX tends to perform poorly when it is paying the VRP while the VIX futures curve is upward-sloping (*in contango* using futures parlance) and tends to perform best when it is receiving VRP while the curve is downward-sloping (*in backwardation*). In other words, VXX has often performed best *after* the VIX has risen toward 20 where the curve usually begins to invert, while the *worst* time to buy is when the VIX is low and the VIX curve is steep.

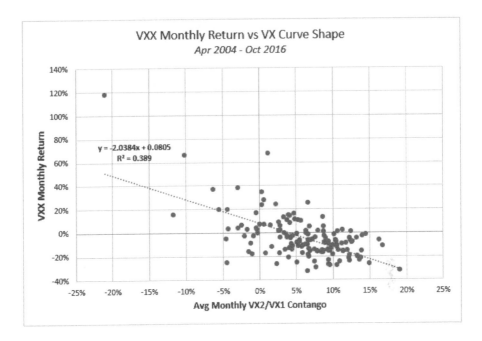

Figure 14.4: VXX performance vs. VIX curve shape.

Crisis Alpha Approaches

With an understanding of the factors affecting VIX derivatives pricing, the need to manage the 'cost of carry' of any long VIX position quickly becomes apparent. While there are nearly infinite variations, cost-conscious crisis alpha positioning in VIX derivatives generally falls into one of two categories: (1) a tactical approach that attempts to find the most effective risk/reward environments to hedge, or (2) the construction of low-cost positions designed to be always carried. As with most investment strategies, each approach has its own trade-offs and the best choice will ultimately depend on an investor's specific circumstances.

Approach 1: Tactical Long VIX

The concept of a *rolling panic* in equity markets can be compared to fighting a forest fire. Often, containing the damage from the initial brush fire is easy and the surrounding environment quickly bounces back. However, occasionally a series of brush fires combine to form a large-scale forest fire, exponentially raising risk and complicating containment efforts, which can ultimately lead to widespread damage and a lengthy recovery period.

The financial market equivalent of a forest fire is an inversion in the VIX term structure. Inversions are caused by high demand for equity hedges (S&P 500 Index options) that drives the price of near-term volatility above longer-term volatility. This occurs because longer-dated volatility pricing typically is anchored by the strong tendency of the VIX index to revert to its long-term average of about 20. This can be seen in the historical ranges and median values in the VIX futures. The farther out the curve, the closer the median values cluster around 20, and the tighter the range around that median (see Figure 14.5).

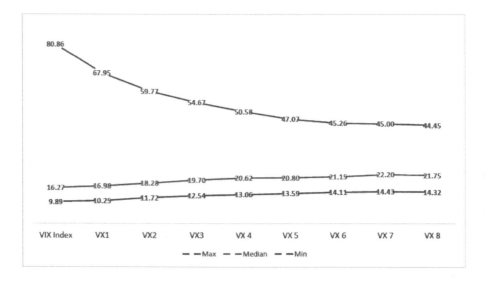

Figure 14.5: VIX and VIX futures historical range, March 2004–November 2016.

Since VIX futures were listed in 2004, an inverted VX curve has been the "gateway" to a crisis; while not *every* inversion has led to a crisis, all major crises have started with an inversion (see Figure 14.6). This fact makes the VIX curve a logical place to look for a tactical signal to apply crisis alpha strategies. While there are many variations, the general approach for this signal is to monitor the price of the VIX index relative to the various VIX futures or among the VIX futures themselves. Whether in real-time or on a slower time frame, an inverted term structure flagged by this calculation would then indicate that a hedging position in VIX futures or options is warranted.

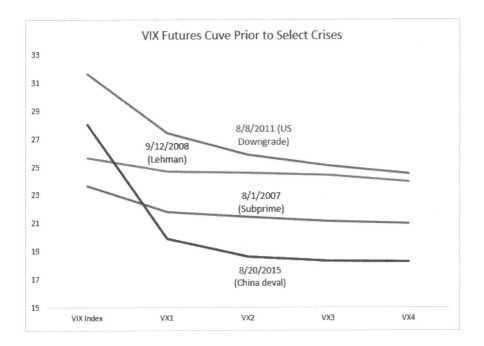

Figure 14.6: VIX futures curve prior to select crises.

Aside from its benefit as a timing signal, an inversion turns the typical cost of carry on its head. While the curve is inverted, time is a *benefit* for long VIX positions as the underlying futures are pulled up toward the VIX index by expiration. In a true crisis, as panic rolls from one asset class to another, keeping the VIX elevated for an extended period, this can be a substantial 'wind at the back' for crisis alpha positions. Under this scenario, the term structure can indeed make the VIX 'cheap' to own, even at 20 or higher.

Pros

Past equity panics have been characterized by a rapid fall in equity indexes such as the S&P 500. The rapidity of decline in combination with the magnitude can cause large moves upward in near-term volatility as market participants struggle to price in new and rapidly changing information. This period of acute uncertainty can be very profitable for a long volatility position as the rapid rise in VIX combined with the *tail wind* from the inverted term structure can result in an exponential rise in VIX futures prices. As an example, the S&P 500 Short Term VIX

Futures Index returned +334% in the 59 days from August 29, 2008 to its peak on November 20, 2008.

Cons

VIX futures term structure inversion is a process; it takes time to manifest itself and is almost always accompanied by some degree of equity market (S&P 500) drawdown prior to inversion. With this understanding, hedging using VIX term structure will almost always be late compared to 'always on' hedges.

High volatility periods and VIX futures curve inversions are an iterative process that develops over days and weeks. "One-off" shocks like the Japanese earthquake and tsunami or the "Flash Crash" in May 2010 can cause large spikes in the VIX index, but are usually transitional and do not lead to inversion beyond a few days. For an investor using inversion as a hedging signal, this leaves the portfolio unhedged at the beginning of most equity drawdowns and subject to false signals.

Approach 2: Low Cost-of-Carry Options Structures

Investors looking for a protective position at all times must be aware of the cost of protection. A cost-conscious position with explosive return characteristics is a VIX 1x2 call spread. Specifically, this position is created by selling 1 out-of-the-money call option to buy 2 further out-of-the-money call options. Typically, the goal is to search for strike price combinations resulting in a very low up-front cost or even a credit in some circumstances.

The VIX *backspread* is an explosive position if owned prior to a large move higher in volatility. With this position, you are long not only the price/level of volatility but also the 'volatility of volatility' (VVIX index) as seen in Figure 14.7. The cost of this position will therefore be highly dependent on the implied volatility level in VIX index options themselves (the VVIX index) as well as the distance between strike prices.

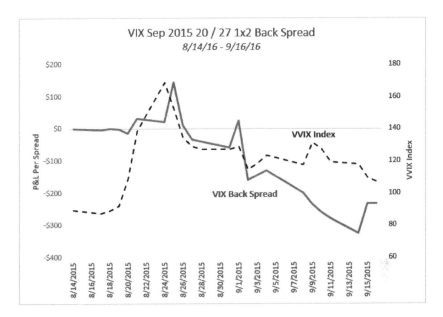

Figure 14.7: VIX 1x2 call backspread, August 2015.

Pros

Due to its explosive potential when the VIX and VVIX index spikes, this position has been described as "banging two sticks of dynamite together." Once a spike in volatility occurs, you also have flexibility to convert the backspread into a butterfly by selling an even further out-of-the-money call, collecting additional premium while holding the position. The position can also be customized by adjusting the distance between strikes to suit your particular outlook or capital requirements.

Cons

This position has margin requirements that need to be taken into consideration before entering it. The August 2015 scenario laid out also demonstrates that this position needs to be managed and adjusted if a volatility event occurs. This is not a "set it and forget it" type of trade. You can lose money in this position if the VIX index settlement ends up above the short strike, but below the long strike.

Exit Strategy

The benchmarks of a high-quality hedging strategy are not only its performance during times of equity market drawdowns, but your ability to know when to stay on the sidelines and when to take profits. Given the historical tendency of equity markets to rise over time, cost minimization and profit-taking are key to a successful crisis alpha strategy.

While VIX futures curve inversion may be a satisfactory entry signal, waiting for full VIX futures curve normalization is not recommended as an exit condition, as this will generally result in a 'round trip' or reversal of any profit from a long volatility position. Systematic profit-taking and position reduction based on levels of the VIX index or stages of curve normalization may provide a more effective way to monetize successful hedge positions. Profit taking based on the duration of term structure inversion may also be advisable. For context, the crisis periods of Fall 2008 and Fall 2011 saw the two longest periods of VIX futures term structure inversion in history, both persisting for about a calendar quarter. A more typical inversion would tend to last only for a matter of days or weeks.

The high VIX index levels benefitting crisis alpha strategies are rare and only provide a brief window of opportunity when they occur. High VIX levels sow the seeds of their own destruction as market participants incorporate new information and market movements fail to justify investors' worst fears. For example, to sustain a level of 40 on the VIX index, equities would technically need to have a daily trading range outside of +/−2.5% in 10 of the next 30 trading days, an exceedingly rare occurrence in stock market history. In the long run, markets are adaptive systems that are not surprised by the same information twice.

Part IV: **Appendices**

Appendix A
Important Terms

Over the course of this book, I have introduced the lingo and jargon of the options industry. There are two goals for this appendix: (1) for you to be able follow along with what I am trying to teach in this book; and (2) to present what I mean when I discuss these topics and to give you an understanding of what they mean to me when I talk about it.

Historical Volatility (HV)

Historical volatility is a backward-looking number. It is a representation of the history of volatility. Historical volatility typically uses a calculation called GARCH (Generalized Autoregressive Conditional Heteroskedasticity) to calculate how much an instrument has moved over a previous period of days. Without getting too deep into the weeds, the GARCH model compares where the underlying closed the previous day relative to where it closed the next day and determines how much the underlying moved. HV uses a set number of days in the GARCH model to calculate volatility over previous days.

GARCH is limited by one major flaw: it only looks at end-of-day pricing. It misses how much an underlying might move throughout the day. If the S&P 500 moves UP 15 points and then down 20 and settles the day up 5, GARCH modelling will only see 5 points of movement. Is that 5 points of movement an accurate way of portraying how much the underlying moved? The answer is no, so while HV is important, it doesn't tell the whole story.

Even so, historical volatility is what tends to drive price perceptions going forward. The assumption is that how volatility moved in the past will be a good indicator of how volatility will move in the future. In betting on how something will move, we tend to look at specific time periods, each meaning different things depending on the amount of data reviewed.

Short-Term Historical Volatility

Short-term HV studies periods existing over less than a month. This means looking at the last 10 trading days, the last 20 trading days, and the last 30 trading days. Figure A.1 shows a graph of the volatility over time.

https://doi.org/10.1515/9781501505676-015

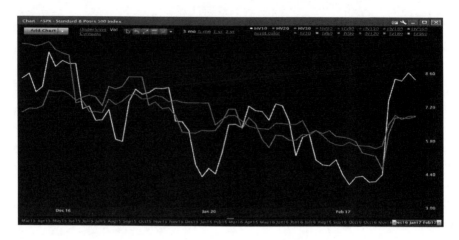

Figure A.1: Short-term Historical Volatility.

HV10 moves much more quickly than 20 day volatility and HV20 moves more than 30 day, although the difference in movement between 20 and 30 is far less than the difference in movement between 10 and 20. Near-dated HV gives you a view of what has happened recently. It tends to miss some intra-day movement. It also tends to be the best view of what might happen next. These should be looked at in three month increments at most.

Intermediate-Term Historical Volatility

If near-dated HV gives you a view of what has been going on recently and what might happen next, *intermediate HV* is going to give you the general trend of movement based on the last 2–6 months. High volatility tends to lead to more volatility and low volatility tends to lead to lower volatility. Looking at intermediate volatility gives you an idea of what the general trend has been on the product over the last few months. It tends to be smoother, but can still anticipate major movement.

A vol trend frees you from some of the noise of near-dated HV. When this hits historic levels, it can mean that the underlying is at a reversal point. Be wary when these numbers are hitting highs or lows, because that can mean the market is setting a trap and is primed for a reversal. In Figure A.2, SPX movement is below 7% over the previous 60 days and below 8% over the previous 90 days, about as low as movement in the S&P 500 will get. I find this type of information invaluable as it helps me see that movement is lacking, at a minimum will not go much lower, and is likely to go higher. When I view movement at historic lows, I know that even if I don't want to buy options, I also do not want to be net short options.

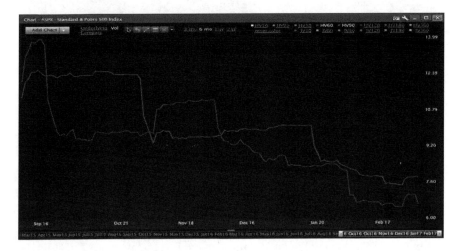

Figure A.2: Intermediate-Term Historical Volatility (HV of 60 and 90 days).

Long-Term Historical Volatility

Long-term HV is meant to point out where the mean reversion point is. Movement is always mean reverting to a point. If movement has been steadily decreasing, as it was in Figure A.2, and mean reversion is in the cards, long-term HV is where you will see the movement unless the underlying is completely breaking out. This reversion level, like a stock's moving average, is dynamic and will act like a resistance point. Consider long-term HV to be a reversion level for the underlying.

180 day vol, shown in the lower graph in Figure A.3, acts as a near term stop for movement and tends to be a resistance point for forward-looking volatility measures. In Figure A.3, the 180 vol is about 11%, pointing toward where near term vol is likely to find resistance if HV increases from the 6% it was trading. 360-day HV can show the true reversion level if an event occurs or movement starts to increase. Yes, the underlying IV might explode higher but, in general, when other vol measures hit HV360 that will be a level where price either goes much higher or turns around.

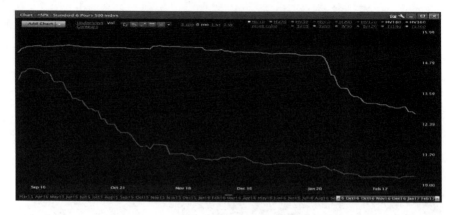

Figure A.3: Long-Term Historical Volatility.

Realized Volatility (RV)

Realized volatility is how the underlying is moving at the moment. This term describes how an underlying moved while you are setting up a trade. It can also be interchangeable with short-term HV. You look at what amounts to HV of 10 to 20 days. For the most part, when I think about realized volatility, I think about 10 day HV.

Looking at Figure A.4, which is 10 day HV, I can describe how the S&P 500 (SPX) has been moving in the recent past, which is the best I can do to describe what is happening right now. While HV10 can say what's happened in the recent past, it can't say what is actually happening right now. This is the one place where something like candlesticks might actually show movement. The candlestick, the pattern seen on most modern charts, shows a great deal of information: High to low (the rectangular 'real body'), trading range extension above and below, and direction (white candles moved up, black candles moved down).

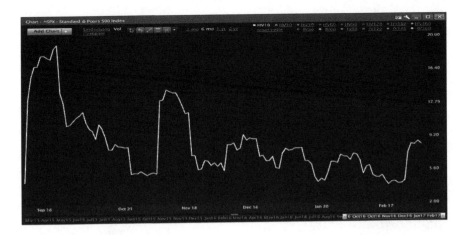

Figure A.4: Realized 10-Day Volatility.

I can see ups and downs on this candlestick chart (Figure A.5). Combined with historical analysis, you can see what is going on with the underlying instrument. In the chart above, in my eyes, the answer is a trend. SPX has slow momentum higher.

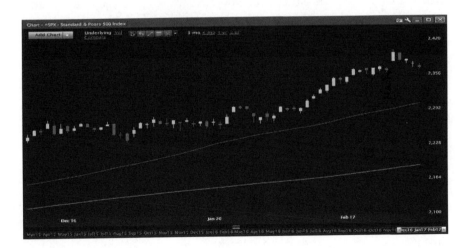

Figure A.5: Candlestick chart.

Forward Volatility

Forward volatility is how much an asset might move going forward over a certain period of time. The options pricing model uses five factors: (1) underlying price, (2) strike price, (3) time to expiration, (4) cost of carry, and (4) forward volatility.

The problem is that no one knows what forward volatility will be. This is what creates option trading opportunities. In this book, you have seen how the ignorance of forward volatility is where all of the trading uncertainty exists. Understanding that forward vol is a moving target allows you to make profitable trades. If forward vol were known, there would be no trading.

Implied Volatility (IV)

Implied volatility is the market's best guess at how volatility will be going forward. While HV is backward facing, IV is forward facing. IV does rely on the past, but it also takes into account what might happen in the future. What is interesting, and a common misconception, is that IV is actually an *output* of the pricing model, not an input.

The pricing model is based on the Black-Scholes formula, used for calculating what an option's price should be *in theory*. While an older model, it is the source for many newer models. Traders use many types of pricing models, but all options models use the following five factors: (1) price of the underlying, (2) strike price of the option, (3) time to expiration of the option, (4) cost of carry, and (5) forward volatility that was originally used in the model developed in Black-Scholes.

This sounds easy, except that we only know four of the five factors. We do not know what forward volatility is going to be. Thus was born implied volatility. IV is derived using what we know: the four factors in the pricing model. Using the options price and the four factors, we run a formula to solve for forward volatility via calculus, creating implied volatility. Implied volatility is an *output* of the pricing model, not an input. Thus, as the factors of the model change or the option's price changes, IV changes. The Greeks are based on IV and can also move based on what happens with the four factors and the option's price. IV is a market-driven number. Here is an example of how that equation for IV looks:

Option Price = Stock Price*Time*Carry*Strike*X Unknown Forward Volatility (IV)

If a $30 stock has an ATM options price of 2.00 with 30 days to expire, a carrying cost of 0.05, and a strike of 30, the formula would be at onset:

2.00=30*30*0.05*30*X

When the market moves IV to an extreme, there is a chance to set up a trade. It depends on whether you think options are fairly priced. IV as seen in VIX moves up and down much like a stock price as shown if Figure A.6.

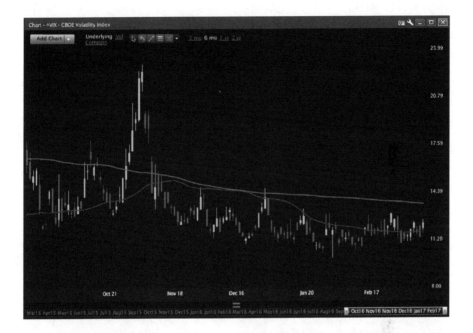

Figure A.6: IV movement.

The only difference between HV and IV is that IV is driven by concepts of mean reversion—the assumption that volatility returns to a mean.

Calls and Puts

An option is a contract that enables you to buy or sell an underlying or an asset at a specific price and time. An option that allows you to buy at a pre-determined price is called a *call. A call option is exercised only when the strike price is below the market price of the underlying, without exception. A put is the opposite. An option that gives the owner the right to sell at a specific price is referred to as a put. A put would be exercised if the strike price is above the market price of the underlying (in the money), without exception.*

Skew

Skew is the relationship between puts and calls as they relate ATM (at the money). It is the formation of volatilities of options below the current price, relative to at-the-money options, relative to options that are above the strike. OTM options trade relative to ATM options' skew. Options are not tied to one another, but they are connected. When ATM IV moves, calls and puts move, but not necessarily at the same rate. When IV falls, the same is true. OTM calls and OTM puts can move free of ATM options. An out-of-the-money call and an out-of-the-money put can gain value whether the ATM options values change or not, especially in indexes and ETFs if a customer that has an axe to grind on a particular option, portion of the curve, or direction of the underlying. Take a look at the skew chart in Figure A.7.

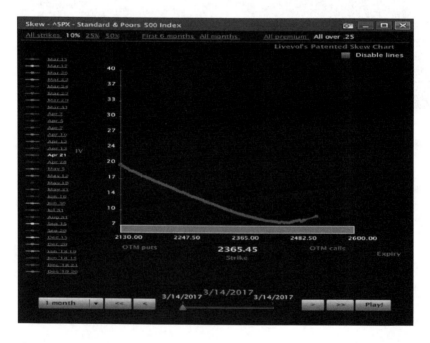

Figure A.7: Skew chart.

SPX, like most indexes, has a higher IV for puts than for calls. However, this curve doesn't remain constant, but moves with changes in the underlying price and also with trade volume in options. While it is hard to see, there are spots where vol is cheap or expensive in relative terms. The dots line up around the 2250 strike in Figure A.7.

Skew can get out of whack. Look at FEZ, a leveraged ETF 2X long on the Eurozone (Figure A.8). The 35 calls are cheaper than the 39 calls even though the 39 calls are OTM. What drove this? Customer call buying. A customer bought 20,000 of the 39 calls in FEZ ahead of this vol set-up.

Here is how to judge skew:
1. Look at skew across many vol scenarios—what does skew look like when volatility is cheap, expensive, and normal?
2. How did skew move as volatility changed? Skew has a pattern. When IV increases skew tends to move in predictable ways, and if it moves away from those patterns there may be a chance to trade.
3. Was there an order that moved skew? Did a buyer or seller move the curve?

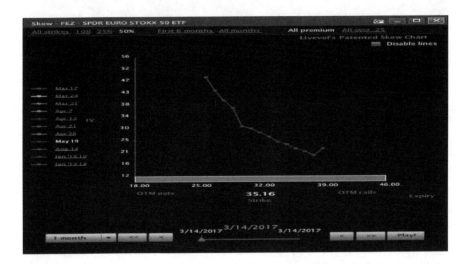

Figure A.8: Skew chart 2.

Looking at the curve above in Figure A.8, we can see where skew went out of whack. In FEZ the 30 puts were more expensive than the 31 or 32 puts. There was likely an order driving up volatility in the May 30 puts. This type of action needs to be evaluated so that you know what is going on, and can potentially find price ranges where you can make money.

Term Structure

While volatility is often presented as a single concept, it is not. Volatility does not move evenly across every contract. While all volatility is correlated, it is not tied at the hip. As skew is created by different demand for different strikes, *term structure* is created by demand for options in different months.

Implied volatility is created by demand; so just as demand is not going to be the same for a given strike, demand will also not be even across different months. In equities, there will be more demand for options during earnings months or when the stock has an important announcement coming. Look at AAPL term structure (Figure A.9). Earnings were predicted as coming up in the term structure below.

Expiry	Mar24(W)	Mar31(W)	Apr07(W)	Apr13(W)	Apr21	Apr28(W)	May19	Jun16
Sigma	15.90	14.78	14.62	14.51	14.39	18.55	20.07	19.29
Sigma Chg	-0.78	-0.48	-0.28	-0.28	-0.27	0.21	-0.34	-0.36
Vol								

Figure A.9: Predicting earnings with term structure.

Based on Figure A.9 above, earnings were unlikely to be announced before April 21st. Less certain was whether earnings would be published after the April 28th contract or sometime before May expire. Earnings before the May contract expire create one scenario; and the April 28 contract had a dramatic increase in IV over April 13. May was higher than the April 28th contract and June showed lower IV than May. This can also be observed in pharmaceutical stocks that have drugs up for FDA review. You can see when the market thinks an FDA decision might occur.

When I was a floor trader, I traded a stock called Sepracor. The company was developing a sleep aid called Lunesta. The FDA committee approval was a moving target; thus, term structure was constantly changing. When it appeared something was imminent, IV would pop, and when that turned out to be nothing, IV would tank. However, the official FDA approval date never moved, it was always a contract that customers wanted to own. I managed the fact that traders wanted to sell me the 'boring months' to buy the 'action months.'

Volatility between months is related, not tied. Order flow (customer de-mand) can drive one month in a different direction than another. This is just the way equity flow runs. Index flow is a touch different but can share similar characteristics.

Index term structure is often driven by events. Take a look at Figure A.10, the S&P 500 a few months before the time of Brexit.

Apr15 SPX 11.31 iv -1.96	May20 SPX 13.83 iv -0.68	Jun17 SPX 15.07 iv -0.52	Jul15 SPX 15.82 iv -0.28

Figure A.10: S&P 500 pre-Brexit.

Even in April the market was pricing some type of event to happen in June or July. That turned out to be the Brexit.

Term structure provides a ton of information:
1. What time period is the market looking for movement?
2. When is the next serious event?
3. What movement is expected between different months?

Used to the trader's advantage, you may be able to develop a trade you think will make money.

Term structure is valuable and crucial in developing calendar spreads, for example. When a month seems mispriced, you can use term structure to develop a trade.

Volatility Index (VIX)

The VIX is the CBOE Volatility index. The VIX represents the calculated value of volatility in SPX options (options on the S&P 500) that expire in 30 days. How does it do this? It's complicated.

The VIX Index looks at the weekly options expiring on the Friday before and after a 30-day time horizon in the SPX and pulls implied volatility from every strike with a bid (traders are at least willing to pay 0.05 for the option). The index is called the "fear gauge" or "fear index," and tends to have a negative correlation to the S&P 500. When the SPX is up, the VIX tends to be down. When the SPX is down, the VIX tends to be up.

We do not like the description of VIX as a fear gauge. We prefer to call it the insurance gauge. The VIX measures how much it costs to insure a portfolio. When the VIX is high, it points to market turmoil. Look at a chart of VIX in Figure A.11.

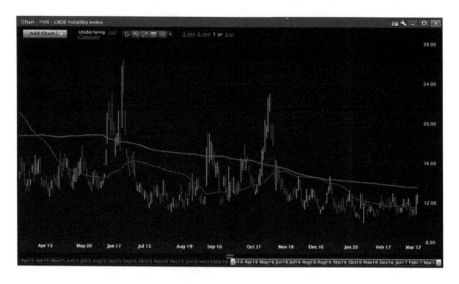

Figure A.11: VIX chart.

When VIX was high, markets were a mess. VIX tends to move before a major event. In the case of Brexit, VIX started to rally two weeks before the vote. It did the same thing ahead of the 2016 presidential election in the U.S.

The VIX index is the baseline for setting volatility across any product that is traded in the equity space. If VIX is low, vol in that equity should lean lower. If it doesn't, that could be a trade.

Delta

Delta is slope. It represents your exposure to directional movement in the underlying stock. If a position expects the underlying to rally, it positively correlates with the underlying. If the position expects the underlying to fall, the position is short delta. An example:

A position is long 100 delta. If the underlying rallies 1 point, the position will make 100.00 (1*100). If the underlying falls one point, the position will lose 100.00 (−1*100).

A position is short 100 delta. If the underlying rallies 1 point, the positions will lose 100 (1*–100). If the underlying falls one point, the position will make 100 (–1*–100).

Delta is directional exposure. If a position will make or lose money based on movement on the underlying, the position has delta. Look at a chart of a long call. With a 0% move, the contract has no P&L, but for every 2% move it picks up about its delta in P&L.

Delta is the red line in Figure A.12. As the underlying rallied in a direction, how does the position perform?

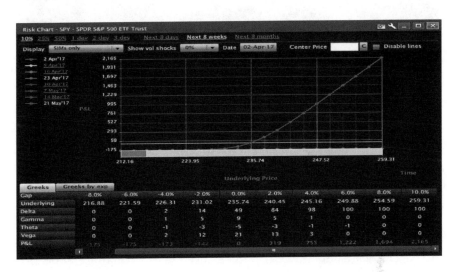

Figure A.12: Delta chart.

Gamma

When you have a position as the underlying moves around, you will see delta change—this degree of change is *gamma*. Gamma is a position's exposure to movement, not in one particular direction, rather movement in *either* direction. Look at a chart of 20HV in the SPX in Figure A.13.

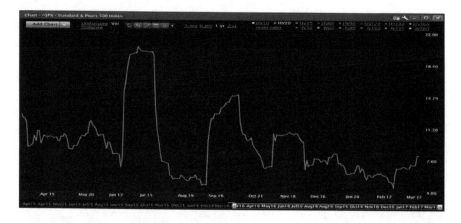

Figure A.13: 20 day HV in SPX.

This movement shows where gamma comes into play. When the SPX starts to move, it measures gamma as a related factor. That occurs often.

A common problem among traders is understanding that the *sign* of gamma has nothing to do with the *sign* of delta. You can have a positive gamma and negative delta and vice versa. What gamma measures is what happens to delta as the underlying moves. If you are short delta and long gamma and the underlying rallies, you become less short delta. If you are short delta and long gamma and the underlying falls, you will become more short delta with exposure to the underlying.

Gamma doesn't directly affect P&L; it affects delta. Following are some examples of the math behind gamma:

- A position is long 100 delta and long 100 gamma and the underling rallies 1 point. The position is now long 200 delta.
- A position is long 100 delta and long 100 gamma and the underlying falls 1 point. The position is now flat delta.
- A position is long 100 delta and short 100 gamma and the underlying rallies 1 point. The position is now flat delta.
- A position is long 100 delta and short 100 gamma and the underlying falls 1 point. The position is now long 200 delta.

Look at the call from above. Delta changes as the underlying rallies in Figure A.14.

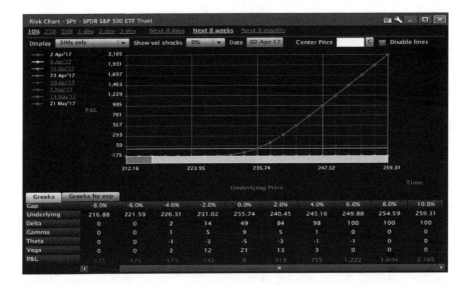

Figure A.14: Delta changes.

At a 0% move, delta was 49. When SPY was up 2%, delta changed to 84. That is the way gamma helps you measure and manage trades. A quick increase in the underlying dramatically changes delta, and that change is gamma.

Theta

Theta represents the position's exposure to time. As a day passes, the theta of a position tells you whether or not you are making money. If a position has theta of positive 100 and a day passes, the position should in theory make $100.00. Look at a chart of option premiums on a long call option in Figure A.15.

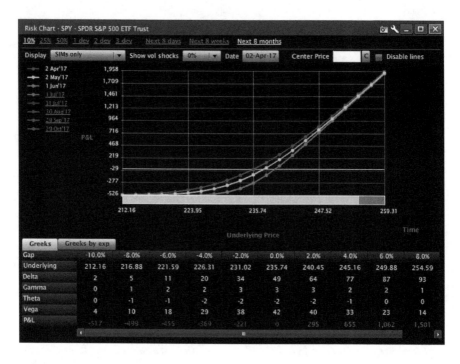

Figure A.15: Multiple payouts in SPX over the life of a call option.

As time passes, ATM options move. The way to measure that cost is theta. Options are like insurance—as time passes, insurance policies lose value, and the loss of insurance value is what theta measures. It works in your favor if you are short premium, and against you when you are long. Think about theta like this:

- A position is long 100 theta and a day passes. Your position should make $100.00.
- A position is short 100 theta and a day passes. Your position should lose $100.00.

Theta is what the position produces in time decay, which is not an easy thing to keep track of over multiple positions and many option trades—unless you manage positions with theta in mind.

Vega

Vega is to volatility as delta is to underlying price. When IV increases, vega reacts to the movement in implied volatility. A one point increase in implied volatility will cause the option position to gain the value of its vega. Look at a chart of the call above with a change in implied volatility in Figure A.16.

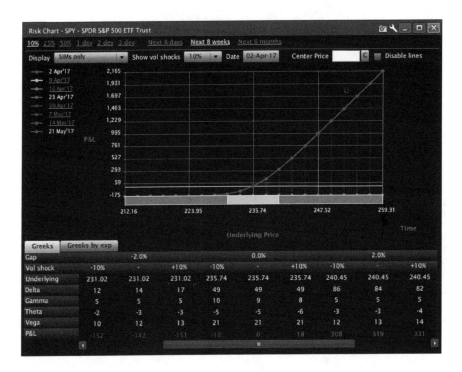

Figure A.16: A call payout in SPX.

If IV rallies 10%, the position makes money. This is directly related to the vega of the position. Negative vega will behave the opposite of the above and is created by short options. Vega, like gamma, moves less as the underlying moves away from the starting price of the trade.

Appendix B
Best Blogs

The set of blogs below is from the Option Pit blog, a blog we keep nearly daily. These are our real-time thoughts and application of concepts to the topics we discussed in this book.

http://www.optionpit.com/node/641198 ("Cheapest volatility on the planet-TWTR that!" 5/28/2015)

http://www.optionpit.com/blog/will-aapl-iv-ever-stop-declining ("Will the AAPL IV ever stop declining?" 4/22/2014)

http://www.optionpit.com/blog/kersplat-goes-implied-volatility-fb-now-what-do ("Kersplat goes the implied volatility in FB now what to do?" 1/15/2013)

http://www.optionpit.com/blog/vix-super-expensive ("VIX is Super Expensive" 8/29/2012)

http://www.optionpit.com/blog/vix-vs-vxgog-forming-trade ("VIX vs VXGOG forming a Trade? 8/27/2012)

http://www.optionpit.com/node/643155 ("Massive Vol Collapse as VIX goes thud" 5/24/2016)

http://www.optionpit.com/node/642822 ("TSLA term structure kinda backward" 3/30/2016)

http://www.optionpit.com/node/642741 ("What was the other side of the VRX trade?" 3/16/2016)

http://www.optionpit.com/node/641533 ("Oil Option Markets Calling a Bottom? 8/3/2015)

http://www.optionpit.com/node/641280 ("Do we get to the 9 handle?" 6/11/2015)

http://www.optionpit.com/node/642864 ("The Never Ending Land of Negative Rates and Monetary Flimminy Flammery" 4/7/2016)

http://www.optionpit.com/node/642430 ("Are Oil and VIX Breaking Up?" 1/25/2016)

https://doi.org/10.1515/9781501505676-016

http://www.optionpit.com/blog/how-would-did-spx-butterfly-perform-if-traded-thursday ("How would did an SPX Butterfly Perform if Traded Thursday?" 9/24/2010)

Index